THE CONSERVATIVE AGENDA

IDEAS in CONFLICT

Gary E. McCuen

publications inc.

411 Mallalieu Drive
Hudson, Wisconsin 54016
Phone (715) 386-7113

Illustration and Photo Credits

The Democratic Socialists of America 85; Steve Kelly 137; Jeff MacNelly 115; Gary Markstein 143; Presidents' Budget Reports 67; Franklin Delano Roosevelt Library 47; Senate Finance Committee 53, 79; Father Robert A. Sirico 29; Sojourners Magazine 19; Ron Swanson 13; U.S. Department of Treasury 73.

© 1996 by Gary E. McCuen Publications, Inc.
411 Mallalieu Drive, Hudson, Wisconsin 54016

publications inc. (715) 386-7113

International Standard Book Number
0-86596-138-7
Printed in the United States of America

CONTENTS

CHAPTER 3   THE ROLE OF GOVERNMENT

REASONING SKILL DEVELOPMENT

These activities may be used as individualized study guides for students in libraries and resource centers or as discussion catalysts in small group and classroom discussions.

IDEAS in CONFLICT

This series features ideas in conflict on political, social, and moral issues. It presents counterpoints, debates, opinions, commentary, and analysis for use in libraries and classrooms. Each title in the series uses one or more of the following basic elements:

Introductions that present an issue overview giving historic background and/or a description of the controversy.

Counterpoints and debates carefully chosen from publications, books, and position papers on the political right and left to help librarians and teachers respond to requests that treatment of public issues be fair and balanced.

Symposiums and forums that go beyond debates that can polarize and oversimplify. These present commentary from across the political spectrum that reflect how complex issues attract many shades of opinion.

A *global* emphasis with foreign perspectives and surveys on various moral questions and political issues that will help readers to place subject matter in a less culture-bound and ethnocentric frame of reference. In an ever-shrinking and interdependent world, understanding and cooperation are essential. Many issues are global in nature and can be effectively dealt with only by common efforts and international understanding.

Reasoning skill study guides and discussion activities provide ready-made tools for helping with critical reading and evaluation of content. The guides and activities deal with one or more of the following:

RECOGNIZING AUTHOR'S POINT OF VIEW

INTERPRETING EDITORIAL CARTOONS

VALUES IN CONFLICT

WHAT IS EDITORIAL BIAS?

WHAT IS SEX BIAS?

WHAT IS POLITICAL BIAS?

WHAT IS ETHNOCENTRIC BIAS?

WHAT IS RACE BIAS?

WHAT IS RELIGIOUS BIAS?

*From across **the political spectrum** varied sources are presented for research projects and classroom discussions. Diverse opinions in the series come from magazines, newspapers, syndicated columnists, books, political speeches, foreign nations, and position papers by corporations and nonprofit institutions.*

About the Editor

Gary E. McCuen is an editor and publisher of anthologies for libraries and discussion materials for schools and colleges. His publications have specialized in social, moral and political conflict. They include books, pamphlets, cassettes, tabloids, filmstrips and simulation games, most of them created from his many years of experience in teaching and educational publishing.

CHAPTER 1

RELIGION AND THE CONSERVATIVE AGENDA

READING

1

THE RELIGIOUS RIGHT: A POLITICAL AGENDA

Ralph Reed

Ralph Reed is the Executive Director of the Christian Coalition, a national organization of more than 1.5 million Americans of Christian faith. Reed delivered this speech before the Detroit Economic Club in January of 1995.

■ **POINTS TO CONSIDER**

1. According to the author, what kind of victory did the 1994 elections represent?

2. Discuss some of Reed's priorities for Congress in the first hundred days and beyond.

3. Contrast what the author sees as the government's treatment of the institution of the family with the Christian Coalition's goals for the family.

4. Why does Reed refer to the Great Society as "a failed experiment in massive social engineering?"

Excerpted from a speech by Ralph Reed before the Detroit Economic Club, January 17, 1995. Reprinted with permission of **Vital Speeches** and The Christian Coalition.

Our goal is not to legislate family values, but to see to it that Washington values families.

The American people and many of you in the business community are still trying to make sense of the new political order ushered in by the 1994 elections...This election signaled the largest single transfer of power from a majority party to a minority party in the twentieth century...

But the election was more than a partisan victory. It was a victory for ideas and ideals. It was a landslide for a particular kind of change: pro-life, pro-family, low-tax, and unapologetically committed to restoring traditional values...Challenged by attacks on their faith, religious conservatives went to the polls in record numbers...It was the largest turnout of religious voters in modern American political history. The results were astonishing. They voted 70 percent Republican and only 26 percent Democrat...

THE FIRST HUNDRED DAYS

Our society — any society — cannot survive when its inner cities resemble Beirut, when children pass through metal detectors into schools that are war zones, when one out of every three children is born out of wedlock, and when one out of every four Americans is functionally illiterate.

Our first step in replacing this older order has already begun. For the next 86 days, we must simply pass the Contract with America. The Christian Coalition will do its part. We will launch the largest single lobbying effort in our history, beginning tomorrow when all fifty of our state chairmen fly to Washington to personally work for passage of the Balanced Budget Amendment. Through phone banks, fax networks, satellite television, computerized bulletin boards, talk radio, and direct mail, we will mobilize our network of 1.5 million members and supporters in 1425 local chapters in support of of the contract. By the time the dust settles, we will spend an estimated $1 million to deluge Capitol Hill with phone calls, faxes, and telegrams. After the votes have been taken, we will distribute over 60 million pieces of literature between now and 1996 informing people of faith how their Congressmen and Senators voted on the Contract — family tax relief, welfare reform, a tougher crime bill, term limits, and real spending cuts.

But there is much more to be done. What will come after the Contract and the first 100 days? It is far too early to predict with certainty what will transpire, but let me suggest four priorities for the new Congress.

PROMOTING FAMILY

First, the government should promote and defend rather than undermine the institution of the family. As a society, we simply cannot survive another 30 years of no-fault divorce and no-conse-quence parenthood. Catholic law theologian Michael Novak has written that the family is the most effective department of health, education and welfare ever conceived. He adds, "If it fails to teach honesty, courage, desire for excellence and a host of basic skills, it is exceedingly difficult for any other agency to make up for its failures."

Our primary task is to take power and money away from government bureaucrats in Washington and return it to parents and children. To this end, we must relieve the crushing tax burden on the American family. The average family of four now spends 38 percent of its income on taxes — more than it spends on food, clothing, housing, and recreation combined. To their credit, the Republicans have proposed a $500 tax credit per child for mid-dle-class working families. That is a good downpayment. But we should go further by tripling or quadrupling the standard deduction for children so that no family of four in America making less than $30,000 pays a dime in federal income tax.

The federal government must no longer subsidize those agencies and programs that promote values contrary to those that we teach in our homes. Taxpayer funding for the National Endowment for the Arts, the National Endowment for the Humanities, and Corporation for Public Broadcasting should end. If we are going to ask single mothers in our inner cities to sacrifice by getting out of the wagon and helping to pull it, it is only fair that we require some sacrifice from the tuxedo and evening pumps crowd.

We should also eliminate taxpayer subsidies that encourage family break-up and the taking of innocent human life. Funding for the Legal Services Corporation, which every year provides tax-payer dollars to pay for 200,000 divorces — more than one out of every three divorces in America — should be reduced. It is tragic enough that one of every two marriages ends in divorce, and that

11

millions of children in our nation have never known a father. It is unconscionable for the federal government to assault the traditional family with our tax dollars.

Our goal is not to legislate family values, but to see to it that Washington values families. The values of faith and family that we advance are cherished in our hearts, taught in our schools, honored in our homes, and celebrated in our churches and synagogues. They are not so weak or insecure that they require any agency of the government to win their converts. But it is not too much to ask the government to be the friend rather than the foe of families.

LIMITING GOVERNMENT

Our second priority is to radically downsize and limit government. The values that we espouse are values that are learned, not mandated. These are the values taught around kitchen tables, and on father's knees, and during prayer meetings, and during midnight mass and Sabbath services. They are values which suffer when weighted down by the heavy hand of government.

Ronald Reagan once said, "The closest thing to eternal life on earth is a federal program."

For some of these programs, the time has come for a decent burial. A good first step would be to eliminate or downgrade several Cabinet departments, including Commerce, Energy, Housing and Urban Development, and Education. In my view, education will be the number one social issue for the remainder of this decade, and abolishing or downgrading the Department of Education will be our top legislative priority. We propose defederalizing education policy by block granting federal functions back to states, locally elected school boards, and parents. Specifically, we will work with Congress to return much of the $33 billion we spend at the federal level — 70 percent of which never reaches the classroom — to the states in the form of matching grants for scholarships or vouchers so that parents can send their children to the best school in their community, whether private, public, or parochial.

CHARITY, NOT WELFARE

Our third priority should be to replace the failed and discredited welfare state with a community and charity-based opportunity

society. For most of our history, welfare was the function of homes, churches, synagogues, and civic associations that practiced "true compassion." This compassionate society was defined by generosity, not by handouts and pity. In this light, the Great Society plan was not a bold new step, but a failed experiment in massive social engineering.

Glenn Loury, a brilliant economist from Boston University, who also happens to have grown up in the inner-city, said recently, "[I]n every community there are agencies of moral and cultural development that seek to shape the ways in which individuals conceive of their duties to themselves, of their obligations to each other, and of their responsibilities before God...If these institutions are not restored, through the devoted agency of the people and not their government, [it] threatens the survival of our republic."

We must replace the pity of bureaucrats with the generosity of churches and synagogues; the destructiveness of handouts with the transforming power of responsibility; the centralized approach of the Great Society with the care of responsive communities and local government.

The federal government spends nearly $200 billion on 436 welfare programs spread out over four Cabinet departments. The current system penalizes work, discourages marriage, punishes the family, and consigns millions to hopeless, multigenerational poverty. It has enslaved the very people it promised to protect. We recommend consolidating most federal welfare programs in the form of block grants and returning them to the states with a few simple, common-sense reforms. Reforms that discourage out-of-wedlock births and encourage work. Reforms that allow private and religious institutions to provide help to mothers and children in need. Reforms that reinvigorate rather than atrophy communities. This block grant scheme should not, however, become just another massive new entitlement. The clear goal should be to eliminate, in the course of the next decade, federal involvement in welfare and shift responsibility to private charities and the faith community.

REAFFIRMING RELIGIOUS LIBERTY

The fourth and final priority of the new Congress should be to secure religious liberty and freedom of conscience for all of our citizens. Too often, a strange hostility and scowling intolerance greets those who bring their private faith into the public square. Consider the following:

In Missouri, a child caught praying silently over lunch was sent to week-long detention. In southern Illinois, a fifteen-year old girl was handcuffed, threatened with mace, and shoved into the back of a police car. Her crime? Praying around the flagpole before school hours...

For us the issue is much broader than voluntary school prayer. Rather, we seek to redress three decades of systematic hostility towards religious expression by government agencies, the schools, and the courts. We will propose a religious liberty statute and constitutional amendment, modeled after the Religious Freedom Restoration Act of 1993, to guarantee the right of all Americans to express their faith without fear of discrimination.

These four priorities — insuring that government is the friend rather than the foe of the family, limiting the size of government, replacing the welfare state with a compassionate society, and securing religious freedom for all — are the embodiment of our legislative agenda. But in the end — and this is important — we will be judged as a movement not by how many precincts we organize, nor by how many bills we pass into law, nor by how many people are elected to office. We will be judged by how we act and by who we are.

14

READING

2

AN ALTERNATIVE TO THE RELIGIOUS RIGHT

Jim Wallis

Jim Wallis is the Editor of Sojourners Magazine, *an Evangelical religious journal of spiritual, social and political commentary. He is also the author of the recent book,* The Soul of Politics: A Practical and Prophetic Vision for Social Change.

■ POINTS TO CONSIDER

1. Contrast the author's definition of evangelical Christianity with the one promoted by the religious right and the media.

2. Analyze what Wallis sees as the failure of the religious right.

3. Discuss, as the author indicates, how both sides of the religious community have perpetuated political polarization.

4. Evaluate the author's belief that the nation faces a spiritual crisis.

Jim Wallis, "Who Speaks for God?" **Sojourners Magazine**, March/April 1995: 16-18. Reprinted with permission from **Sojourners**, 2401 15th Street N.W., Washington, D.C. 20009; (202) 328-8842.

Prophetic religion is subverted when wealth and power are extolled rather than held accountable; when the gospel message is turned upside-down to bring more comfort to those on the top of society than to those at the bottom.

Who speaks for God today? The Religious Right would have us believe that it does. The media have been very cooperative, giving right-wing fundamentalists most of the coverage when the issues of politics and religion come up. And religion and politics come up all the time these days.

For several years now, the Religious Right has virtually controlled the national discussion of politics and morality with the help of the media, who have virtually ignored alternative voices. And with all its money, the Religious Right literally has been able to buy its own microphones and broadcast its message around the world. The time has come to challenge the Religious Right and offer a deeper perspective. A clear, visible, public alternative is vitally needed today — one that lifts up another vision of the relationship between faith and politics.

NEW CONVERSATION

Among many sectors of the church's life, a new conversation is taking place. Dissenting evangelical voices seek a biblical approach to politics, not the ideological agenda being advanced by the Religious Right. Strong Catholic voices assert their own church's social teachings as a vital alternative to the Religious Right and the secular Left. Many African-American, Latino, Asian, and Native American church voices combine personal and family values with a commitment to social justice that leads them to embrace neither the liberal nor the conservative program. New voices from all the Protestant churches feel represented neither by old religious liberalism nor Religious Right fundamentalism.

Together, we proclaim an evangelical, biblical, and catholic faith that must address a nation in crisis; and we will not be dismissed as "liberals" or "secular humanists" as the Religious Right always characterizes those who disagree with it. We do not challenge the Religious Right's "right" to bring its religious values into the public square as some political liberals have. On the contrary, we believe that our impoverished political process needs the moral direction and energy that spiritual and religious values can

16

contribute to the public debate. Separation of church and state rightly prevents the official establishment of any religion but does not and must not prohibit the positive influence of religious communities on the nation's moral and political climate.

The question is not whether religious faith should make a political contribution, but how. If religious values are to influence the public arena, they ought to make our political discourse more honest, moral, civil, and spiritually sensitive, especially to those without the voice and power to be fairly represented. That is where the Religious Right has failed. Since the 1980s, the powerful influence of the Religious Right has been an important factor in making our political debate even more divisive, polarized, and less sensitive to the poor and dispossessed.

MEANING OF FAITH

At stake is not just politics, but the meaning of faith itself. It is time to challenge the aggressive right-wing litmus test that has distorted the independent moral conscience that faith can bring to politics. Many committed Christians are dismayed by those who would undermine the integrity of religious conviction that does not conform to a narrow ideological agenda. And prophetic religion is subverted when wealth and power are extolled rather than held accountable; when the gospel message is turned upside-down to bring more comfort to those on the top of society than to those at the bottom.

Regrettably, the Religious Right has claimed the evangelical faith and an almost exclusive right to define it by its political agenda. That reality has become especially problematic for the many evangelical Christians who do not endorse the political Right. In fact, most evangelical Christians are not members of the Religious Right, despite the media-created perception of an evangelical right-wing juggernaut. Even the word "evangelical" has become so identified with a particular political and cultural militancy that many evangelical Christians now hesitate to identify themselves as such.

"Evangelical" used to be a good word. It means a biblically rooted and Jesus-centered faith, and it comes from the word "evangel" — meaning "good news." Jesus himself used the word to announce the meaning of his coming. There, standing in the temple in the little town of Nazareth, he quoted Isaiah's ancient prophecy, "The Spirit of the Lord is upon me, because he has

17

anointed me to preach good news [the evangel] to the poor..."

The Religious Right preaches a politics that is more nationalist than truly evangelical. Listening to its leaders' words and agenda, one hears little about Jesus at all. Their political preference for wealth, power, and military might flies in the face of a gospel that was intended to be good news to the poor and was preached by an itinerant Jewish rabbi who said that it was the peacemakers who would be blessed.

EVANGELICAL CHRISTIANS

One wonders whether the Religious Right even knows its own history. In the last century, evangelical Christians were leaders in the abolitionist movement against slavery, were tireless advocates of the poor and oppressed, and were in the forefront of the struggle for women's rights. Is today's Religious Right agenda good news to the poor, women, and disadvantaged racial communities?

The evangelical Christian movement has been hijacked. Evangelical Christianity has been commandeered by a combination of fundamentalist preachers and right-wing political operatives who recognized their common cause and the power to be gained by taking over the evangelical label. They have now effectively done so in the perception of the nation.

True evangelical faith focuses on the moral values that must be recovered to heal the torn political fabric; ideological faith would rend the fabric further in the pursuit of power. Evangelical faith tries to find common ground between warring factions by taking the public discourse to higher ground; ideological faith fuels the rhetoric of "us and them" and breeds a climate for hate and even violence. Evangelical faith holds up the virtues of compassion and community; ideological faith appeals to personal and group self-interest. Evangelical faith understands religious faith as a call to humility and reconciliation rather than the basis for attacking those who are less righteous.

POLITICAL VISION

Who will articulate a political vision that seeks common ground between diverse people with legitimate concerns? The politics of division will only take us lower and lower. We need a politics of values and vision today, one that takes seriously both personal and social transformation.

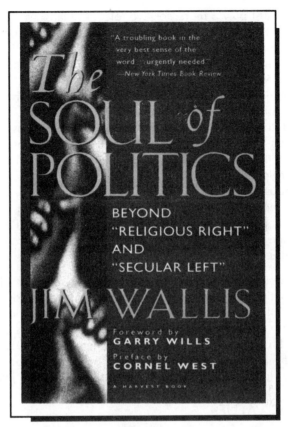

In the *Soul of Politics*, Jim Wallis writes about the relationship between religion and politics from the perspective of the evangelical Left in American religious life.

Despite public cynicism, a deep longing exists in the land for rediscovering the moral heart of our public debate. Many Americans now believe the crisis we face is a spiritual one, and deeper than politics as usual. It's the "healing of the nation," as envisioned by the biblical prophets, that we most need today, and the "soul" of politics that we must recover. While the liberals and conservatives carry on arguments that seem more and more irrelevant and relentlessly attack each other, our children are being shot in the streets.

Our times cry out for renewed political vision. And vision depends upon spirited values. But if politics will be renewed more by moral values than by partisan warfare, the religious community must play a more positive role. The language of morality and faith is absolutely essential to political discourse. Because the crisis we face is spiritual, it must be addressed by solutions that address the "spirit" of the times that often lies beneath our political and economic problems. Further, the old political language and solutions of Right and Left, liberal and conservative are now almost completely dysfunctional and helpless to lead us into a different future. Conformity to the old options offered by either the Religious Right or the Religious Left will not take us forward. The almost total identification of the Religious Right with the new conservative political rulers in Washington, D.C., is merely the latest dangerous liaison of religion with political power. Such faith is clearly more ideological than truly evangelical. With the ascendancy and influence of the Christian Right in the Republican Party, the religious critique of power has been replaced with the religious competition for power.

Likewise, the continuing identification of religious liberalism with political liberalism and the Democratic Party has demonstrated a public witness without either moral imagination or prophetic integrity. Liberal religious leaders have sought access and influence with those in power no less than their Religious Right counterparts. Neither right-wing religious nationalism nor left-wing religious lobbying will serve us at this critical historical juncture...

MORAL VALUES

Many of us care deeply about moral values and the breakdown of family life. We feel the erosion of personal responsibility and character in our neighborhoods and nation. But that doesn't lead us into the arms of the Religious Right. On the contrary. We believe that social responsibility is also at the heart of our biblical traditions, that racism and sexism are also sins, and that the best test of a nation's righteousness is not its gross national product and military firepower but, according to the prophets, how it treats the poorest and most vulnerable.

WELFARE POLICY DEBATE: THE POINT

Don Reeves

Don Reeves is an Economic Policy Analyst. He wrote the following piece for Bread for the World, *a nationwide Christian movement active in promoting awareness of hunger issues. The organization also promotes federal funding of programs that help to feed hungry people.*

■ POINTS TO CONSIDER

1. Summarize what the author calls the "cliff" effect for former welfare recipients.

2. Compare what Reeves feels is essential in overcoming poverty with the functions of the current system.

3. Restate the figures the author cites for the AFDC programs.

4. Describe the systematic economic factors that the author credits as contributors to societal breakdown.

Don Reeves, "The Welfare Policy Debate," **Bread for the World Newsletter,** May, 1995.

*Seventy percent of the families who go on welfare
leave in less than two years. Only seven percent of
AFDC families stay in the program longer than eight
years. The average is 2.3 years. Most leave because
they go to work.*

Throughout biblical history, God commands the community
and its civil and religious leaders to render justice for poor and
hungry people. From Exodus through the Prophets and into the
New Testament, God's intent is to establish justice on the earth
and to judge the nations on how they treat people in need.
Whether it be Moses addressing Pharaoh or Jesus recounting the
parable of the Good Samaritan, advocating justice for poor and
oppressed people is a fundamental component of the scriptures.
In biblical terms, justice means more than acting in a fair and
honest manner. It means making sure that vulnerable people get
what they need to live.

Those of us who believe that God has been more than fair with
us are moved to work for social justice. As citizens of a democracy, we can help shape government policies that are just and fair to
everyone, particularly to poor people.

BROADENING THE WELFARE REFORM DEBATE

Welfare generally, and in this paper specifically, refers to Aid to
Families with Dependent Children (AFDC), the joint federal-state
program of cash payments to poor families — usually single-
parent households.

In the current national debate, the term "welfare" refers to a
broader range of assistance programs being considered for cuts.
The "welfare reform" package passed by the Republican-con-
trolled House of Representatives in March 1995 would reduce
and revamp programs for food stamps, school meals and other
nutrition programs, supplemental security income, child care, foster care and child support, in addition to AFDC. The projected
savings in the federal budget would total $66 billion over five
years (some $30 billion from nutrition programs alone). All
together, however, these programs which focus on meeting minimal needs of poor families are but a fraction of the public transfers
to U.S. citizens and businesses which might be called welfare.

If U.S. government policies toward poor and hungry people are
to become more effective, the discussion must be broadened still

22

further — to include education and work skills, employment and wage policies, health care and a range of community services, particularly child care. All of these are key to helping families move out of poverty.

AFDC AS A SUCCESS, AS A FAILURE

"If it weren't for AFDC, I would not have been able to go to college and get my degree," says Caron Brinkley, a 22 year-old registered nurse in South Dakota. Caron became a mother at age 16. "I got married two weeks before my son's birth. But when his father decided to go back on alcohol and drugs, I wouldn't have him in the house. Our son was too important to have that around. So I went on AFDC and went to college."

Now Caron works as a home visiting nurse for teen mothers.

AFDC was created during the 1930s to provide a minimal bridge across family emergencies, most often at that time due to the death or departure of the male wage earner. Together with food stamps, Medicaid and housing assistance for some, AFDC continues to serve that purpose for most recipients. Seventy percent of the families who go on welfare leave in less than two years. Only seven percent of AFDC families stay in the program longer than eight years. The average is 2.3 years. Most leave because they go to work. About one-third of AFDC recipients will be on welfare for two or more periods during their lifetimes.

Even though long-term recipients are a small minority among all AFDC recipients, they account for a majority of the cost of the program, are regarded as "typical" welfare families and are the focus of the current welfare reform debate. But many long-term recipients are not employable, often because of the physical condition of the parent or of a child in the family. AFDC, food stamps and Medicaid may in fact be less expensive than institutional or other alternatives in caring for unemployable people.

Insofar as welfare has failed, it is not the failure of the AFDC program alone, or even primarily. More systematic problems include the failure of the economy to create sufficient opportunities for workers to support their families at a decent level, inadequate health care, lack of affordable housing, racism and other biases, and lack of quality child care. These failures contribute, in turn, to family breakdown and the inability of families and schools to help children fully develop their potential. Responsible welfare reform must address this larger complex of problems.

23

The current welfare debate risks destroying AFDC's relative success — the minimal "bridge" it provides for most participants — while failing to address the underlying problems of long-term participants.

REFORMS TO OVERCOME HUNGER AND POVERTY

The goal for anti-poverty policy reform should be to help people, particularly children, out of poverty. Responsible anti-poverty reform should adhere to the following principles.

Creating Secure Livelihoods

Requirements or successful encouragement for welfare parents to earn their own livelihood must be accompanied by investment in improving job skills and habits, an increase in job availability and earnings or wage supplements that enable a decent standard of living. Long-term welfare recipients are often ill-equipped to compete for jobs, particularly in a job market characterized by falling real wages, high unemployment rates, little job security and limited benefits, especially health care coverage.

Time limits for receiving welfare will not do much to get people into jobs unless the people have job skills and good jobs are available. Public employment can add some job opportunities. But if "workfare" simply bumps people already employed from their jobs, there is no net gain.

Getting the Incentives Right

A major flaw in present welfare programs, and many reform proposals, is the "cliff" effect. A welfare recipient who takes a job usually suffers a drop in standard of living, most often the abrupt loss of Medicaid (since few entry level jobs include health care coverage). One way of "making work pay" is to reduce the rate at which assistance is taken away when a family becomes employed. A complementary approach would be health care assistance for all low-income families, regardless of employment, and access to affordable, quality child care. Increasing the earned income tax credit, which supplements the income of working poor families, would also enhance the benefits of low-wage jobs.

A second perverse effect of AFDC rules is that benefits are available mainly to single parents, reinforcing an unfortunate societal trend. Schemes targeted on raising the income of intact families above the poverty line could help reverse this incentive.

WELFARE MYTHS

Welfare Is an Attractive Life Style

Purchasing power of AFDC benefits plus food stamps for a three-person family declined 27 percent between 1972 and 1993...

Welfare Rolls Keep Expanding

As a proportion of poor families, AFDC recipients have actually declined. Between 1973 and 1990, the number of people on welfare stayed roughly constant, fluctuating between 10.3 and 11.4 million people, rising during recessions and falling as the economy recovered...However, the number of people in poverty has risen from 25 million in 1970 to 39 million in 1993. Therefore the program serves a falling share of poor people...

Welfare Increases Single-Parent Families

Single-parent families have increased among all income groups. In fact, the increase in single-parent households has been slightly faster in non-poor than poor families, and birth rates to unmarried mothers are generally higher in states with lower, rather than higher AFDC benefits — both contrary to the argument that welfare leads to more out-of-wedlock births....

Welfare Reform Will Help Balance the Budget

Potential savings from welfare reform are slight, at best. In 1993, total AFDC costs (federal and state) were $25.2 billion. The federal share was $13.8 billion, less than 1 percent of total federal expenditures.

"Welfare Myths," **Bread for the World Background Paper, No. 133**, May 1995.

Community Support Services

Juggling the demands of job and home is difficult enough for two-parent families with middle incomes. But when there are no funds for repair, a broken down car is a crisis, not just an inconve-

nience. Child care and other work expenses, especially health care, can take away much of what a single parent can earn. If a parent works longer hours, the children may join the ranks of "latchkey" kids. So if we are going to require work by single parents, we must take into account the demands of single parenting on a shoestring budget. Low-income families will need affordable, quality child care.

Maintaining an Adequate Safety Net

Allowing one fifth of our country's children to grow up in poverty is morally unacceptable, unfair to the children, and false economy in the long term for the whole society. Families who work for pay, and those who do not but who need assistance and fulfill reasonable expectations of public assistance programs, should be lifted above the poverty line. Proven tools include the minimum wage, earned income tax credit, cash assistance, food and supplemental nutrition programs, housing assistance and health care assurance.

Meanwhile, it is quite feasible to end widespread hunger in this country within two or three years by adequately funding the federal food programs — mainly food stamps, school meals and the Special Supplemental Food Program for Women, Infants, and Children (WIC) — which work. There is no excuse for the hunger that is so widespread in this country, especially among children.

Re-establishing Community

The current welfare reform debate is scapegoating low-income families. The debate is also feeding racial, ethnic and gender biases. Legal immigrants who are not citizens are now a target too, even though they contribute to the economy and pay taxes. Some participants in any government program (including programs for the affluent and defense contracts) will abuse the system, so safeguards are necessary. But the welfare reform debate is focusing criticism mainly on those receiving assistance, rather than on the lack of jobs paying decent wages and the inadequacies of our present assistance programs.

READING

4

WELFARE POLICY DEBATE: THE COUNTERPOINT

Robert A. Sirico

Paulist Father Robert A. Sirico is President of the Acton Institute for the Study of Religion and Liberty (161 Ottowa Ave., N.W, Suite 301, Grand Rapids, Michigan 49503. Tel.: 616-454-3080). The Acton Institute is a non-profit, non-political, interfaith organization founded to promote an understanding of the moral foundations of the free market among religious leaders.

■ POINTS TO CONSIDER

1. Restate what Father Sirico finds to be the "fundamental flaw" in the welfare system.

2. Contrast the top-down and "subsidiarity" approaches in aiding the poor. What is subsidiarity?

3. What would be the result of eliminating the federal government's role in welfare policy?

4. Summarize some of the steps Father Sirico cites that would increase private charitable giving.

Excerpted from the testimony of Father Robert A. Sirico, before the U.S. House Agricultural Subcommittee on Department Operations, Nutrition and Foreign Agriculture, February 1995.

To the extent that the federal government is the major player in the field of welfare, its secular agencies drive out the moral influence of religious mediating institutions.

No society can call itself civilized or moral that does not have a concern for the poor and vulnerable among us. Indeed, it could be said that the test for a moral society is how it affects those most in need. Are there opportunities for the disadvantaged to become independent by using their God given right to work? Are they able to keep the fruits of their own labor? How are those most in need — through no fault of their own — treated by others? How well does the society preserve its fundamental unit: the family? These are the criteria for a morally healthy society. If these are the standards by which the morality of a society is to be judged, then I am sorry to report to you something I believe you each already know: We have failed.

WELFARE AND POVERTY

It is my contention that the way we have gone about meeting the needs of the poor and disenfranchised is an impractical and often wrong-headed way. Our national strategies for welfare have attempted to help the individual person in need from the most distant and bureaucratic level: the federal government. The result has been a system that tends to lump all the poor in one class. Yet in reality poor people are individuals — with different situations, talents, resources, and weaknesses. From the lofty plane of Washington's welfare bureaucracies, the poor have been treated as a mass in need of new policies, initiatives, and programs. In truth they are radically heterogeneous individuals with specific requirements that are too subtle to be discerned from this city.

In my view, the other fundamental flaw of our welfare system is that it has subsidized the very problems it was intended to solve. It has been some thirty years since the establishment of the Great Society and billions of dollars have been extracted from the American people to fund it. Yet illegitimacy, family breakdown, drug abuse, crime, gang activity, welfare dependency, and teenage pregnancy are worse. Despite the good intentions of welfare-state promoters, like some of the 19th century's medical practices, the cure has proven worse than the disease.

28

Father Robert A. Sirico

I am not here as a public policy expert. However, I do have wide experience working with private charities, including AIDS hospices, medical clinics, soup kitchens, homes for unwed mothers, hospitals for the elderly and infirm, to name a few. I have witnessed much suffering and pain on the part of those in need. I came here today to suggest to you ways to think about how our society should address poverty.

There is an alternative to the top-down approach to welfare. There is a simple principle which I believe should guide the direction of welfare reform. The principle to which I allude is known as *subsidiarity*, which holds that those social functions that can be accomplished by a lower order of society should not be taken over by a higher order. Thus, when it comes to the administration of relief to the poor, those closest to the person in need ought to be the resources of first resort. The federal government should be the resource of last resort — to be turned to only in situations that cannot be accomplished by more local bodies.

Some will say that local agencies and institutions cannot effectively meet the needs of the poor, that they are not large enough, funded sufficiently or motivated enough. My reply is to ask that you consider the impact of the inverse of the principle of subsidiarity on the mediating institutions. Using government as the resource of first resort lessens the incentive of people at the local level to become involved in needed projects. In economic jargon this works like Gresham's law: Bad charity drives out good charity.

Federal intervention has become the norm in providing for the needy. Let us at least agree that this needs to be altered to the point where federal intervention is the exception rather than the rule, and to where it intervenes only when emergency situations arise, and then only in such a way that the actions of society itself (as distinct from the state) are not thereby impeded.

WELFARE AND RELIGION

To the extent that the federal government is the major player in the field of welfare, its secular agencies drive out the moral influence of religious mediating institutions. These religious institutions — when unhampered by state and federal regulations — provide a critical moral atmosphere that stretch the client to become as independent as possible. Individual caregivers dealing personally with the poor also encourage moral renewal. In many cases, this is a dramatic transformation of the individual, from a state of moral weakness to strength, dependence to independence. Such a transformation often requires hard work on the client's part and many will reject it if an easier alternative is provided through government programs.

In my experience, the charities that have been most successful have been those that rely — in large part — on the voluntary efforts of people who really care. They invest of their own time and resources in projects in their own communities. From this proximity — where a servant of the poor is able to see the face and hear the voice of the needy person — he or she is far more capable of fulfilling needs that are spiritual and emotional — as well as material. They have come to have an intimate awareness of a client's situation and they have the greatest incentive to meet those needs.

WEED PULLING

An African proverb states "poverty makes a free man become a slave." Programs like AFDC, combined with food stamps and housing assistance, although meant for good, have broken up more families than slavery ever did. As a result of these broken families, children are being raised without fathers in the home. This single fact contributes more than anything to the chaotic atmosphere in America. The downward spiral of poverty is the root for many of our country's ailments. The deeper the root grows, the more crime, drugs, illegitimacy and illiteracy sprout like uncontrollable weeds. As a child, I remember watching my mother pull weeds in the yard. Congress needs to weed pull and spend the necessary time on shaping an effective welfare program that encourages an upward spiral out of poverty and starves the ailments. Even Aristotle and Marcus Aurelius knew in their days that "poverty is the mother of crime."

Excerpted from testimony of Larry Jones of *Feed the Children* before the House Ways and Means Committee, January 30, 1995.

RELIGION AND GOVERNMENT

I am frustrated by the apparent inability of many in the mainstream religious leadership to see a simple truth: If Congress reduces its role in this area, it would open a wide arena for our institutions to play an even greater role in forming the moral atmosphere of segments of our society desperately in need of such a transformation.

Another sensitive point of concern should be noted. The federal government has subsidized many of the private religious charities that have historically provided the finest care to the indigent. When this happens, the flexibility of private charities, essential in enabling these agencies to reach out where the human need is greatest, is lost. The charities become less adaptable in difficult circumstances.

Funding to private religious charities also puts into play a host of political concerns that the charities did not have to concern themselves with previously. Slowly, agencies that began with the intention of serving those in need, begin to look for ways in which the government can aid them in doing this, and tend to rely less on charitable donations. Eventually their role may change from servant of the poor to lobbyist for an ever expanding welfare state. They may even find themselves dependent on the federal government for their very existence. Energy, money, and creativity that could be used to solve social problems is spent on lobbying activities. How can such agencies be expected to help others out of dependence when they themselves are caught in the snare?

You can help religious institutions live up to their potential. I hope you will avoid the temptation to believe that the welfare system can be merely tinkered with to be successful. The goal for Congress should be to remove the impediments to private charity and keep federal programs from competing with them. I am not a policy expert, but I do know that people give more to charity when they are taxed less. Your goal should be to shift the burden of welfare from citizens, in their role as taxpayers, to citizens in their role as good people with charitable hearts, assisted by professionals who can do the work without excessive government regulations. Nearly 90 million Americans volunteer at least three hours a week at a non-profit. They will do much more — and give more — if they know they are needed.

Furthermore, I would encourage you to take steps to make charitable giving more financially rewarding. Proposals have been suggested which would allow individuals to deduct 110 percent of their charitable contributions, thereby increasing their incentive to give. Or you could replace the charitable tax deduction with a tax credit, which would allow people to support whichever charitable organizations they deem most effective. These questions are for you to decide, but as you deliberate consider changes that would help your own friends and family become better givers.

PRIVATE CHARITY

Now if private charity is allowed to assume a greater role, will people fall through the social safety net? The short answer is yes. Yet they are also falling through the cracks in the present statist, centralized system. We cannot create a utopia, a perfect world in which poverty and suffering do not exist. There will always be people who need our care. But our goal should be to create a system that is most adept at finding those who need our help, meeting their authentic needs, and — where possible — helping

32

them to a life of independence. To this end the government system has failed. Now the responsibility must be returned to its proper owners — private individuals and private organizations.

The first task for political leaders dedicated to promoting real reform requires humility. Because before private charities can be liberated to do what they do best, government officials must admit that the myriad of individuals and institutions in America can handle our welfare problems effectively. The greatest leaders among you will realize that the question should not be "What can government do?" but "What can the American people do without it?"

WHAT IS RELIGIOUS BIAS?

This activity may be used as an individualized study guide for students in libraries and resource centers or as a discussion catalyst in small group and classroom discussions.

Many readers are unaware that written material usually expresses an opinion or bias. The skill to read with insight and understanding requires the ability to detect different kinds of bias. **Political bias, race bias, sex bias, ethnocentric bias** and **religious bias** are five basic kinds of opinions expressed in editorials and literature that attempt to persuade. This activity will focus on religious bias defined in the glossary below.

Five Kinds of Editorial Opinion or Bias

Sex Bias – the expression of dislike for and/or feeling of superiority over a person because of gender or sexual preference

Race Bias – the expression of dislike for and/or feeling of superiority over a racial group

Ethnocentric Bias – the expression of a belief that one's own group, race, religion, culture or nation is superior. Ethnocentric persons judge others by their own standards and values.

Political Bias – the expression of opinions and attitudes about government-related issues on the local, state, national or international level

Religious Bias – the expression of a religious belief or attitude

---

Guidelines

Read through the following statements and decide which ones represent **religious bias**. Evaluate each statement by using the method indicated below.

- **Mark (R)** for any statements that reflect religious bias.

- **Mark (F)** for any factual statements.

- **Mark (O)** for any statements of opinion that reflect other kinds of opinion or bias.

- **Mark (N)** for any statements that you are not sure about.

1. _____Allowing one fifth of our country's children to grow up in poverty is morally unacceptable.

2. _____A priority of Congress should be to secure religious liberty and freedom of conscience for all our citizens.

3. _____The goal for anti-poverty policy reform should be to help people out of poverty.

4. _____The 1994 election was a landslide victory for a particular kind of change: pro-life, pro-family, low-tax and unapologetically committed to restoring traditional family values.

5. _____Bad charity drives out good charity.

6. _____Jews should not be allowed a prominent voice in the political discourse because their teachings are not as complete as those of the Christian majority.

7. _____The government should promote and defend rather than undermine the institution of the family.

8. _____The Contract with America grew out of the desires of the Christian majority in America.

9. _____Christian Evangelicals are more intolerant than other religious groups.

10. _____Religious institutions will live up to their potential when they stop relying on the government for support.

11. _____The test for a moral society is how it affects those most in need.

12. _____The federal government should be the resource of last resort.

13. _____Most Catholics are overconcerned with the issue of abortion, causing them to lose focus on more important public policy issues.

14. _____The Religious Right teaches a politics that is more nationalist than truly evangelical.

15. _____True evangelical faith focuses on the moral values that must be recovered to heal the torn political fabric.

16. _____The language of morality and faith is absolutely essential to political discourse.

17. _____Throughout biblical history, God commands the community and its civil and religious leaders to render justice for poor and hungry people.

18. _____The current political discourse is too infiltrated by right-wing religious groups.

19. _____The stability of the country depends upon the response of the religious community in the public sector.

Other Activities

1. Locate three examples of religious opinion or bias in the readings from Chapter One.

2. Make up one sentence statements that would be an example of each of the following: **sex bias, race bias, ethnocentric bias**, and **religious bias.**

CHAPTER 2

THE ECONOMIC REVOLUTION

READING

5

THE CONTRACT WITH AMERICA

John C. Goodman

John C. Goodman is president of the National Center for Policy Analysis, a public research institute with offices in Dallas and Washington, D.C., that promotes conservative ideas in political and economic affairs.

■ POINTS TO CONSIDER

1. Evaluate what the author sees as the most "painless" means to reduce the deficit.

2. Analyze the problem with taxing investment income. List alternatives to current policy.

3. Assess the benefit of increasing the Social Security earnings limit for elderly Americans.

John C. Goodman, "Republican 'Contract' Will Boost Economy," December, 1994. Reprinted by permission of the National Center for Policy Analysis, 12655 N. Central Expressway, Suite 720, Dallas, Texas 75243, (214-386-6272).

Nothing will reduce the deficit more efficiently and more painlessly than a higher rate of economic growth.

If the word "mandate" means anything, the Republicans have a mandate to enact their "Contract with America." Before the 1994 election, more than 300 Republicans gathered on the steps of the Capitol to sign the contract, a list of 10 specific bills they pledged to bring to a floor vote in the first 100 days of the 104th session of Congress, if voters gave them a majority in the House of Representatives.

President Clinton and Democratic candidates claimed that the Republican tax cuts combined with a balanced budget amendment would necessitate massive cuts in Social Security. The voters rejected that claim, and they were right to do so.

REDUCING THE DEFICIT

Nothing will reduce the deficit more efficiently and more painlessly than a higher rate of economic growth. And six of the 10 proposals in the contract are specifically aimed at promoting growth and creating jobs. They would increase the U.S. growth rate by two full percentage points over the next five years. Gary and Aldona Robbins, two former U.S. Treasury economists, estimate that at the higher income levels (which higher growth produces), government revenues will increase by $623 billion between now and the year 2000.

That means the Republicans should have little difficulty achieving their other goals. They can enact a $500 per child tax credit, remove the marriage penalty, increase defense spending modestly and still cut the deficit almost in half in the year 2000 — without any decrease in government spending.

The Republican pro-growth proposals are not new. The package is similar to the one recommended to President Bush by the National Center for Policy Analysis (NCPA) and the U.S. Chamber of Commerce in 1991. Bush rejected the package and lost his job. If Clinton accepts the package, he might keep his. Let's see why.

• **Expanding individual retirement accounts (IRAs).** The contract would allow every American to contribute up to $2,000 a year to a "backended" IRA, under which deposits would be made with after-tax dollars, but withdrawals at retirement would be tax-free. Moreover, people with an ordinary IRA could pay taxes on their deposit and transfer the funds to a backended IRA.

This option is important because the average American can expect to face higher marginal tax rates in retirement than during the working years. Not only would this IRA proposal not cost the government any tax revenue, but it would probably increase revenues by $50 billion between 1995 and 2000, as people paid taxes on their current IRA deposits in order to switch to backended accounts.

• **Cutting the capital gains tax.** The debate is over and the verdict is in on capital gains taxes. The 40 percent rate hike in 1986 caused government revenue to go down, not up. In fact, capital gains realizations are lower today (in real terms) than they were in 1985. To stimulate investment and increase government revenue at the same time, the contract proposes excluding 50 percent of capital gains from taxation and indexing capital gains for inflation.

• **Indexing depreciation.** The failure of the tax code to index depreciation schedules for inflation is devastating for manufacturing and other industries that require long-term investments. If inflation averages, say, five percent per year, the value of the depreciation deduction is equal to only one-half the cost of an asset with an eight-year life. To correct this problem, the contract would allow businesses to increase their depreciation expenses each year to reflect the effects of inflation and the time value of money. This change would allow companies to write off the full present value of the cost of productive assets and make choices among different investments based on economic considerations rather than tax considerations.

This proposal for "neutral cost recovery," first advanced by Jack Kemp when he was in Congress, is rarely discussed. Yet in terms of its impact on investment, it is worth all the other proposals combined. The proposal also would provide an immediate incentive without any loss of federal revenue. In fact, tax revenue would increase initially because although firms could increase their depreciation expenses eventually, they would be allowed less depreciation of assets in the first year.

• **Reducing the Social Security benefits tax.** The Social Security benefits tax is not really a tax on benefits. Instead, it is mainly a tax on investment income. No tax is paid unless a tax-

CONTRACT WITH AMERICA

1. The Fiscal Responsibility Act. *A balanced budget/tax limitation amendment and a legislative line-item veto to restore fiscal responsibility to an out-of-control Congress, requiring them to live under the same budget constraints as families and businesses.*

2. The Taking Back Our Streets Act. *An anti-crime package including stronger truth-in-sentencing, "good faith" exclusionary rule exemptions, effective death penalty provisions, and cuts in social spending from this summer's "crime" bill to fund prison construction and additional law enforcement to keep people secure in their neighborhoods and kids safe in their schools.*

3. The Personal Responsibility Act. *Discourage illegitimacy and teen pregnancy by prohibiting welfare to minor mothers and denying increased AFDC for additional children while on welfare, cut spending for welfare programs, and enact a tough two-years-and-out provision with work requirements to promote individual responsibility.*

4. The Family Reinforcement Act. *Child support enforcement, tax incentives for adoption, strengthening rights of parents in their children's education, stronger child pornography laws, and an elderly dependent care tax credit to reinforce the central role of families in American society.*

5. The American Dream Restoration Act. *A $500 per child tax credit, begin repeal of the marriage tax penalty, and creation of American Dream Savings Accounts to provide middle class tax relief.*

6. The National Security Restoration Act. *No U.S. troops under U.N. command and restoration of the essential parts of our national security funding to strengthen our national defense and maintain our credibility around the world.*

7. The Senior Citizens Fairness Act. *Raise the Social Security earnings limit which currently forces seniors out of the work force, repeal the 1993 tax hikes on Social Security benefits and provide tax incentives for private long-term care insurance to let older Americans keep more of what they have earned over the years.*

8. The Job Creation and Wage Enhancement Act. *Small business incentives, capital gains cut and indexation, strengthening the Regulatory Flexibility Act and unfunded mandate reform to create jobs and raise worker wages.*

9. The Common Sense Legal Reform Act. *"Loser pays" laws, reasonable limits on punitive damages and reform of product liability laws to stem the endless tide of litigation.*

10. The Citizen Legislature Act. *A first-ever vote on term limits to replace career politicians with citizen legislators.*

Excerpted from the House Republican Conference "Contract with America."

payer's income reaches a certain level. Beyond that point, the tax rises as income rises. Since 85 cents of benefits is taxed for each additional $1 of income, elderly taxpayers pay taxes on $1.85 for each additional dollar of income. As a result, taxpayers in the 28 percent bracket now face a marginal tax rate of 51.8 percent.

Before 1993, Social Security recipients were taxed on half of their benefits. In 1993, the taxable amount was raised to 85 percent for single people with $34,000 or more and married couples with $44,000 or more in income. The contract would phase out the 1993 changes, dropping it back to 50 percent by 1999.

• **Increasing the Social Security earnings limit.** People between the ages of 65 and 70 who receive Social Security benefits would be allowed to earn up to $30,000 without penalty. Currently, if they earn more than $11,160 in a year, they lose $1 in benefits for every $3 in earnings. When combined with other taxes, this results in a marginal tax rate of more than 100 percent for some older workers. Raising the amount that retirees can earn without loss of benefits would expand the supply of elderly workers, help employers meet their demands for skilled labor over the next decade and increase federal revenue, as additional work-related taxes more than offset increased benefit payments.

• **Increasing the estate tax credit.** The first $600,000 of an estate has been excluded from tax since 1987. As incomes and asset values have risen, the tax is reaching the estates of more middle-income taxpayers. Therefore, the contract would increase the exclusion to $750,000 in 1995 and index it for inflation thereafter.

CONCLUSION

If the effects of increased investment are ignored, the Congressional Budget Office's "static" estimates imply that making these six changes would reduce federal revenue by $150 billion over five years. However, the Robinses have calculated the dynamic — as opposed to static — effects. Using a very reliable estimating method, they conclude that the measures would increase gross domestic product cumulatively by $3.9 trillion by the end of the decade and create an additional 3.2 million jobs.

That's an investment worth making.

A COVENANT WITH AMERICA

Franklin D. Roosevelt and Ronald V. Dellums

Franklin Delano Roosevelt, 32nd President of the U.S., delivered this State of the Union address in January, 1944. Roosevelt and his administration are most noted for designing and implementing the New Deal Programs in the Great Depression of the 1930s. Ronald V. Dellums currently represents the 9th Congressional District of California. He is one of the leading progressive voices in the House of Representatives.

■ POINTS TO CONSIDER

1. Compare and contrast President Roosevelt's 1944 Economic Bill of Rights with Congressman Dellums' 1995 "A Living Wage, Jobs for All" Bill.

2. Summarize President Roosevelt's motivation in introducing a domestic Economic Bill of Rights during a time of war.

3. Discuss Congressman Dellums' reasons, more than fifty years later, for expanding upon FDR's vision of an Economic Bill of Rights.

Excerpted from the State of the Union address of Franklin Delano Roosevelt, "Unless There Is Security Here at Home, There Cannot Be Lasting Peace in the World," January 11, 1944 and from statements of Ronald V. Dellums to his constituents concerning the 1995 "A Living Wage, Jobs for All" Bill.

It is our duty now to begin to lay the plans and determine the strategy for the winning of a lasting peace and the establishment of an American standard of living higher than ever before known. We cannot be content, no matter how high that general standard of living may be, if some fraction of our people — whether it be one-third or one-fifth or one-tenth — is ill-fed, ill-clothed, ill-housed, and insecure.

This Republic had its beginning, and grew to its present strength, under the protection of certain inalienable political rights — among them the right of free speech, free press, free worship, trial by jury, freedom from unreasonable searches and seizures. They were our rights to life and liberty. As our Nation has grown in size and stature, however — as our industrial economy expanded — these political rights proved inadequate to assure us equality in the pursuit of happiness.

An Economic Bill of Rights

We have come to a clear realization of the fact that true individual freedom cannot exist without economic security and independence. "Necessitous men are not free men." People who are hungry and out of a job are the stuff of which dictatorships are made. In our day these economic truths have become accepted as self-evident. We have accepted, so to speak, a second Bill of Rights under which a new basis of security and prosperity can be established for all — regardless of station, race, or creed.

Among these are:

• The right to a useful and remunerative job in the industries or shops or farms or mines of the Nation;

• The right to earn enough to provide adequate food and clothing and recreation;

• The right of every farmer to raise and sell his products at a return which will give him and his family a decent living;

• The right of every businessman, large and small, to trade in an atmosphere of freedom from unfair competition and domination by monopolies at home or abroad;

- The right of every family to a decent home;

- The right to adequate medical care and the opportunity to achieve and enjoy good health;

- The right to adequate protection from the economic fears of old age, sickness, accident, and unemployment;

- The right to a good education.

All of these rights spell security. And after this war is won we must be prepared to move forward, in the implementation of these rights, to new goals of human happiness and well-being. America's own rightful place in the world depends in large part upon how fully these and similar rights have been carried into practice for our citizens. For unless there is security here at home there cannot be lasting peace in the world.

One of the great American industrialists of our day — a man who has rendered yeoman service to his country in this crisis — recently emphasized the grave dangers of "rightist reaction" in this Nation. All clear-thinking businessmen share his concern. Indeed, if such reaction should develop — if history were to repeat itself and we were to return to the so-called "normalcy" of the 1920s — then it is certain that even though we shall have conquered our enemies on the battlefields abroad, we shall have yielded to the spirit of Fascism here at home.

I ask the Congress to explore the means for implementing this economic bill of rights — for it is definitely the responsibility of the Congress so to do. Many of these problems are already before committees of the Congress in the form of proposed legislation. I shall from time to time communicate with the Congress with respect to these and further proposals. In the event that no adequate program of progress is evolved, I am certain that the Nation will be conscious of the fact.

Our fighting men abroad — and their families at home — expect such a program and have the right to insist upon it. It is to their demands that this Government should pay heed rather than to the whining demands of selfish pressure groups who seek to feather their nests while young Americans are dying.

Let me note that the number of this bill, 1050, reminds us that this February, when we reintroduced the act, marks the 50th anniversary of the Roosevelt-Truman Full Employment Bill of 1945. A year earlier, President Roosevelt proposed an Economic Bill of Rights for all Americans, which included the right to work for all Americans willing and able to work. I can only hope that we will not repeat the suffering of the Great Depression of the 1930's before we acknowledge the need for the vision and the goal of the rights stated in that declaration and restated in H.R. 1050.

H.R. 1050 is a call to our historical sense of justice and fairness. It goes beyond the weaknesses of the 1945 Employment Act, builds on the richness of FDR's vision, and presents programs which are desperately needed but cannot be enacted without broad public understanding and support.

We need to build a movement with muscle and a legislative program to prepare the way for a Democratic Party platform that will help elect a new Congress and a Democratic President committed to reversing the damage inflicted during the Reagan-Bush-Gingrich-Dole years. We also need grassroots progressive action in all neighborhoods, towns, cities and counties of the country.

"A Living Wage, Jobs for All" bill is designed to promote, not replace such efforts. We would like to think that the Jobs for All bill can be an umbrella under which ideas can crystallize. This measure is powerful and readable. It should be made available to all labor union members in the country and potentially, be the central pillar of any liberal and progressive organization's program.

Full Employment

We all know that we have expanded in the last two decades a "permanent underclass" of unemployed and seemingly, unemployable people. Unacceptable as this is, we are now in the process of pushing our vast middle class, the strength and bulk of our nation, into a state of job and income insecurity as well.

Business Week, in its cover story on INEQUALITY, subtitled, "How the Gap Between Rich and Poor Hurts the Economy,"

46

Franklin Delano Roosevelt

makes the connections between the increasing gap between the top 25% and the bottom 25% of our society and how this damages salaries and job growth. We don't have to be helpless in the face of this growing trend. In fact, we have an opportunity and an obligation to attempt to reverse this pattern. "A LIVING WAGE, JOBS FOR ALL ACT" is a vision statement that reaffirms FDR'S 1944 declaration of an "Economic Bill of Rights" which, among other economic rights, called for the guarantee of a job for everyone willing to work.

In addition to stating every U.S. citizen's right to work at a decent wage, the bill would also mandate Congress and the President to work together to insure that all federal programs enhance job opportunities. This bill is a call to our historical sense of justice and fairness; it is a call to the richness of FDR's vision and the hopes and aspirations of a generation which had known the Great Depression. We need to reclaim that vision and to declare that we are not victims, but are in control of our destiny.

This is a significant bill for us to consider. The largest societal problem that we have today, greater than our fear about crime, is our fear that our jobs are not secure and that competition for jobs will increase. One of the basic needs in our lives is a job which will pay us a living wage. For most, security and well being flows from the first paycheck that we receive. With a paycheck we become adult, responsible, independent, and able to move on to take on other responsibilities of citizenship and family.

For those of us with jobs, we know that corporate managers, always working towards greater efficiency, prove their competence with savings in payroll through massive layoffs. NAFA and GATT will accelerate the continuing loss of jobs to countries with cheap labor. There is no reason to believe that these basic trends will change in our favor.

It is unrealistic to expect that corporations, which are only market oriented, will take the responsibility for a healthy, national economy. Only we, the people, through our common action, can accomplish this. We need to realize the power of our joint action and take responsibility for our future. This bill is a step in that direction.

A Brief Summary of A LIVING WAGE, JOBS FOR ALL ACT, H.R. 1050

This is a policy measure designed to help nurture an activist movement based on high ideals of democratic human rights and responsibilities. Written in non-legalistic language, it can be easily read by anyone interested in combating the plagues of joblessness, underemployment, economic insecurity, reduced benefits, and poverty.

The bill's major sections suggest a sweeping new jobs for all program going far beyond the original Roosevelt-Truman Full Employment Bill of 1945, the compromise Employment Act of 1946, and the original Hawkins-Humphrey proposals of 1974, before they were watered down.

A Transformation

Without authorizing any additional funds, this proposal would

48

mandate the transformation of the entire U.S. budget of more than $1.5 trillion into a jobs for all budget. This would replace the current ideological commitment to smoke and mirrors budget reduction. With less jobless and poor people receiving transfer payments and more people paying taxes, the deficit would be reduced. Any government borrowing would be used mainly to finance long-term investments in the country's future.

Our bill is a call to our historical sense of justice and fairness. We need to reclaim the richness of FDR's vision without nourishing unrealistic expectations. One of the most important functions of Congress is to help educate the American people. We look forward to doing this, and in the process educating ourselves on the requirements of a Jobs for All Society.

LABOR CRISIS IN THE INFORMATION AGE

Jeremy Rifkin

Jeremy Rifkin is the president of the Foundation on Economic Trends in Washington, D.C. He is the author of The End of Work: The Decline of the Global Labor Force and the Dawn of the Post Market Era. *The following article appeared in the May-June 1995 issue of* Tikkun *magazine.*

■ **POINTS TO CONSIDER**

1. Discuss the "darker reality" of changing labor force patterns.

2. Summarize what Rifkin sees as an ignored discourse, by both right and left, in discussion of the Information Age.

3. Discuss the potential role of the Third Sector in the Information Age.

4. Contrast the philosophy of Third Sector work with that of the traditional "producer and consumer" characterization of labor.

5. Describe some of the incentives for government to promote and fund Third Sector employment opportunities in the twenty-first century.

Jeremy Rifkin, "High Tech Populism in the Information Age," **Tikkun**, May-June, 1995.

Up to now, politicians refused to address the seminal economic and social issue of the next several decades — what to do with the millions of people whose labor is needed less, or not at all, in an ever-more automated global economy.

Immediately following the November elections that swept the Republicans into power in the U.S. Congress for the first time since 1952, pollsters asked voters in focus groups why they switched their party allegiance so abruptly...Sensing that an enormous shift is taking place in the economy, millions of Americans are beginning to worry that there may not be a place for them in the new high-tech Information Age. Talk of balancing budgets, imposing term limits on Congress, and ending unfunded mandates does little to address the underlying concerns of a workforce plagued by declining real wages, dead-end jobs, part-time temporary employment, and long-term structural unemployment.

Concern over diminishing jobs in a changing economy is being voiced with increasing frequency in Congress and in state legislatures, as politicians turn their attention to the welfare issue. While there is general agreement among the leaders of both political parties that welfare benefits must be limited in duration and that all able-bodied people must be retrained for jobs, neither Republicans nor Democrats have bothered to ask the more fundamental question: What jobs?

We are long overdue for a political debate in this country — and indeed around the world — over how best to address the profound changes taking place in the nature of work as we make the transition into the Information Age. That debate should include a discussion of alternative ways of defining human worth now that the commodity value of most people's labor is diminishing in an ever-more automated global marketplace.

THE DAWN OF A NEW ECONOMIC ERA

After years of wishful forecasts and false starts, the new computer and communications technologies are finally making an impact on the workplace and the economy, throwing the world community into the grip of a third industrial revolution. Information Age technologies are already eliminating entire employment categories. Many jobs are never coming back. Blue collar workers, secretaries, receptionists, clerical workers, sales clerks, bank tellers, telephone operators, librarians, wholesalers, and middle managers are just a few of the many occupations destined for virtual extinction.

Although recent government reports claim that unemployment in the United States has declined slightly, they conceal a darker reality. New technologies and corporate re-engineering have displaced millions of American workers, who now labor at low-wage, dead-end jobs, or as temporary employees without benefits. Millions of others have become so discouraged that they have ceased looking for work and therefore go uncounted in the official unemployment figures. More than 15 percent of the American people are currently living below the poverty level.

Earlier industrial technologies replaced the physical power of human labor, substituting machines for body and brawn. The new computer-based technologies, however, promise a replacement of the human mind itself, substituting thinking machines for human beings across the spectrum of economic activity. The implications are profound and far-reaching. To begin with, more than 75 percent of the labor force in most industrial nations engage in work comprised of little more than simple repetitive tasks. Automated machinery, robots, and increasingly sophisticated computers can perform many, if not most, of these jobs. In the United States alone, that means that in the years ahead more than 90 million jobs in a labor force of 124 million are potentially vulnerable to replacement by machines. With current surveys showing that fewer than five percent of companies around the world have even begun to make the transition to the new machine culture, massive unemployment of a kind never before experienced seems all but inevitable in the coming decades.

Of course, market optimists continue to argue that the new technologies of the Information Age will pave the way for an array of new products and services that will create even more jobs...The reality is that the world is polarizing into two potentially irreconcilable forces — on one side, an information elite that controls and manages the high-tech global economy; and on the other, a growing number of permanently displaced workers with few prospects and little hope for meaningful employment in an increasingly automated world. While the knowledge sector and new markets abroad will create some new jobs, they will be far too few to absorb the millions of people displaced by the new technologies of the high-tech revolution.

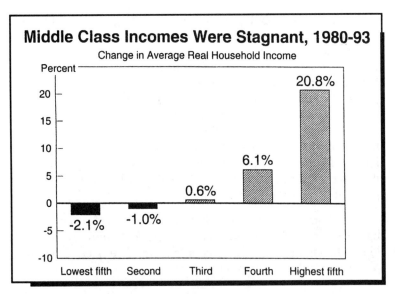

Middle Class Incomes Were Stagnant, 1980-93

Change in Average Real Household Income

Percent

-2.1%	-1.0%	0.6%	6.1%	20.8%
Lowest fifth	Second	Third	Fourth	Highest fifth

Source: Senate Finance Committee, February 8, 1995.

Up to now, the politicians in both the Democratic and Republican parties have steadfastly refused to address what is likely to be the seminal economic and social issue of the next several decades — what to do with the millions of people whose labor is needed less, or not at all, in an ever-more automated global economy. Instead, they have gushed over the great technological breakthroughs that are driving us ever faster into the world of cyberspace and issued breathless pronouncements on the wonders that await us along the information superhighway.

While both Newt Gingrich and President Clinton have embraced the Information Age, extolling the virtues of cyberspace and virtual reality, the Left's response has been to continue to fight a rear-guard action, targeting ideological issues and concerns of a bygone industrial era. In this respect, the Left's current profile bears a striking likeness to the populists of the turn of the century, who fought to maintain an agrarian culture that was quickly being subsumed by the forces of urbanization and industrialization.

In the meantime, few intellectuals and even fewer activists have seriously examined the critical issues raised by the Information Era — especially the question of how to ensure that the dramatic productivity gains of the new high-tech global economy will be shared broadly among every segment of the population. A fair and equitable distribution of the productivity gains would require a dramatic shortening of the work week in countries around the world and a concerted effort by central governments to provide alternative employment in the Third Sector, or social economy, for those workers whose labor is no longer needed in the marketplace. If, however, the dramatic productivity gains of the high-tech revolution are not shared, but rather used primarily to enhance corporate profit to the exclusive benefit of stockholders, top corporate managers, and the emerging elite of high-tech knowledge workers, chances are that the growing gap between the haves and the have-nots of the world will lead to social and political upheaval on a global scale.

What is required now is a bold new social vision and broad-based political movement that can speak directly to the challenges facing us in the new economic era. We need a high-tech populism for the Information Age.

THE THIRTY-HOUR WORK WEEK

To begin with, the business community and elected officials ought to focus serious attention on shortening the work week to thirty hours by the year 2005. The new technologies, after all, were supposed to free us for greater leisure, not longer unemployment lines. In the Industrial Era, when new technologies boosted productivity and reduced labor requirements, working people organized and demanded their right to share in the gains with shorter work weeks and better pay and benefits. Much of the impetus for the five-day work week at the beginning of this century came from the Jewish community. Particularly in the clothing and textile unions, Jewish labor leaders argued that productivity gains ought to be shared with millions of working Americans by reducing the work week from six to five days — allowing a day of rest on Saturday, the Jewish Sabbath.

Today, reformers around the world are beginning to call for a thirty-hour work week to bring schedules in line with the new productive potential of Information Age technologies...

THE THIRD SECTOR AND THE POLITICS OF MEANING

With the need for mass labor diminishing in an increasingly automated global economy, new opportunities for engaging human labor become possible. Unfortunately, we have become so used to thinking of ourselves almost exclusively as producers and consumers that the very idea of creating a revolutionary new context for human activity seems almost fanciful. Yet, we are at the moment in world history when machine technology can begin to substitute for human toil in the production of goods and delivery of services. Large numbers of people are being freed from the production process. Whether that emancipation from the marketplace leads to chronic unemployment, the increasing polarization of rich and poor, and class warfare on a global scale, or a renaissance of the human spirit and a transformation of consciousness largely depends on whether a new populist movement can combine the demand for economic justice with a call for a new way of living in the world. This is the critical juncture where the "politics of materialism" and the "politics of meaning" join together to create a powerful new paradigm for a post-market era.

The first question to ask is what do we do with the increasing numbers of people whose labor is simply not needed in the marketplace, even with a reduced work week. It is unrealistic to believe that the local, state, and federal governments will continue to act as employers of last resort, as they have for the past half-century. In the wake of mounting debts and deficits, government, at every level, can be expected to downsize and diminish in the years ahead. With both the marketplace and government playing a reduced role in the work lives of millions of Americans, the Third Sector, or non-profit community, becomes the last best hope for both restoring the work life of the country and creating a new politics of meaning that can move our society into a post-market era.

For more than 200 years, Third Sector activity has shaped the American experience. While historians are quick to credit the market and government sectors with America's greatness, the Third Sector has played an equally aggressive role in defining the American way of life. The nation's first schools and colleges, its hospitals, social service organizations, fraternal orders, women's clubs, youth organizations, civil rights groups, social justice organizations, conservation and environmental protection groups, animal welfare organizations, theaters, orchestras, art galleries, libraries, museums, civic associations, community development organizations, neighborhood advisory councils, volunteer fire departments, and civilian security patrols are all creatures of the Third Sector...

The Third Sector cuts a wide swath through society. Non-profit activities run the gamut from social services to health care, education and research, the arts, religion, and advocacy. The sector is made up of millions of volunteers as well as paid employees. There are currently more than 1,400,000 non-profit organizations in the United States with total combined assets of more than $500 billion. A study conducted by Yale economist Gabriel Rudney in the 1980s estimated that the expenditures of America's non-profit and voluntary organizations exceeded the gross domestic product of all but seven nations in the world. The non-profit sector already contributes more than six percent of the Gross Domestic Product and is responsible for 10.5 percent of the total national employment. More people are employed in Third Sector organizations than work in the construction, electronics, transportation, or textile and apparel industries.

Today, non-profit and voluntary organizations are serving millions of Americans in every neighborhood and community. Their reach and scope often eclipse both the private and public sector, touching and affecting the lives of every American, often more profoundly than the forces of the marketplace or the agencies and bureaucracies of government...

The market vision, wedded to a materialistic cornucopia, glorifies production principles and efficiency standards as the primary means of advancing happiness. As long as people's primary identification is with the market economy, the values of expanded production and unlimited consumption will continue to influence personal behavior. People will continue to think of themselves, first and foremost, as "consumers" of goods and services.

The Third Sector vision offers a much needed antidote to the materialism that has so dominated twentieth-century industrial thinking. While workers in the private sector are motivated by material gain and view security in terms of increased consumption, Third Sector participants are motivated by service to others and view security in terms of strengthened personal relationships and a sense of grounding in the larger community.

The third sector's role is likely to increase significantly in the years ahead for the simple reason that many of the tasks performed in this sector involve intimate social skills that are not easily reducible to computerization. Ironically, what we have come to think of as high-status skills in the marketplace — even professional jobs requiring years of training — are often reducible at least in part, to digitization and automation. Already, sophisticated information technologies are replacing many of the conventional tasks of engineers, architects, managers, accountants, lawyers, and even physicians. On the other hand, many of the skills we've traditionally relegated to the bottom of the economic pyramid and treated as low-status occupations are far too complex to be replaced by computers and robotization. The skills of an adult-care worker managing a day-care center and nurturing the lives of twenty children are far too complex to be subsumed by the new technologies. In the coming decades, we are likely to witness a profound shift in what we regard as "meaningful" work, as market skills become more automated and intimate people skills in the Third Sector become more valued...

FINANCING A THIRD-SECTOR INCOME

Paying for income vouchers and for re-education and training programs to prepare men and women for a career of community service in the Third Sector would require significant government funds. Some of the money could come from savings produced by gradually replacing many of the current welfare programs with direct payments to persons performing community-service work. Government funds could also be freed up by discontinuing costly subsidies and tax breaks to corporations that have outgrown their domestic commitments and now operate internationally.

Cutting unnecessary defense programs could free up additional funds. Despite the fact that the Cold War is over, the federal government continues to maintain a bloated defense budget. While Congress has scaled down defense appropriations in recent years, military expenditures are expected to run at about 89 percent of Cold War spending between 1994 and 1998...

Perhaps the most equitable and far-reaching approach to raising the needed funds would be to enact a value-added tax (VAT) on all high-tech goods and services. While the VAT is a new and untried idea in the United States, it has been adopted by fifty-nine countries, including virtually every major European nation. By enacting a VAT of between five and seven percent on all high-tech goods and services, the federal government could generate billions of dollars of additional revenue — more than what would be required to finance a social wage for those willing to work in the Third Sector.

Vested interests as well as the new Republican majority in Congress and in many of the state legislatures are likely to resist the idea of providing a social wage in return for community service. Yet, the alternative — leaving the problem of long-term technological unemployment unattended — would create far more onerous burdens for our society. A growing underclass of permanently unemployable Americans could lead to widespread social unrest, increased violence, escalating crime and incarceration, and the further disintegration of American society. Eventually, society will have to ask whether it makes more sense to spend approximately $30,000 per head to keep millions of people in jail each year, or use those same funds for job retraining and income vouchers so that people can find meaningly work in non-profit organizations in the Third Sector, servicing their neighborhoods and restoring their communities.

In the debate over how best to divide up the benefits of productivity advances brought on by the new high-tech global economy, we must ultimately grapple with an elementary question of economic justice. Put simply, does every member of society, even the poorest among us, have a right to participate in and benefit from the productivity gains of the information and communication technology revolutions? If the answer is yes, then some form of compensation will have to be made to the increasing number of unemployed whose labor will be needed less, or not at all, in the new high-tech automated world of the twenty-first century.

Reprinted from TIKKUN MAGAZINE, A BI-MONTHLY JEWISH CRITIQUE OF POLITICS, CULTURE, AND SOCIETY. Subscriptions are $31.00 per year from Tikkun, 251 West 100th Street, 5th floor, New York, NY 10025.

READING

8

HOPE, GROWTH AND JOBS IN THE INFORMATION AGE

Robert S. Walker

Robert S. Walker is a Congressman representing Pennsylvania's sixteenth district. He is a prominent conservative spokesperson in the House of Representatives.

■ POINTS TO CONSIDER

1. Summarize the author's definition of the "Third Wave."

2. Contrast the trends of "Second Wave" Industries with those of "Third Wave."

3. Discuss the role that the author feels the Federal government should play in the Information Age and Third Wave Industry.

4. Analyze the purpose and benefits, according to Walker, of restructuring the Cabinet.

Excerpted from the testimony of the Honorable Robert S. Walker before the House-Senate Joint Economic Committee, June 12, 1995.

Economic change can open vast new horizons of growth and employment.

Since the end of the Cold War we have been struggling to define the best application of government resources to carry forward the technological process made necessary by our national strategy during the Cold War era. We need to create an opportunity for every American by leading the transformation to a Third Wave, Information Age Society that will be the growth of a global economy. The Information Age will create opportunities in a wide range of areas: computer, worldwide electronics, molecular medicine, breakthroughs in material technology, exploring and manufacturing in space, microminiaturization, and virtual reality.

BUSINESS IN THE INFORMATION AGE

A space-based economy is the economy of our future, the Third Wave future. We will be living and manufacturing in space. American will no longer look at space as alien but as the new frontier. We will see economic development of space by using free market principles espoused by commercial providers. We will be working together to create strategies and ideas that will make us respond in ways that enhance America's lead in space and aeronautical research.

We are also looking at a knowledge-based society, a society that is actively involved in the information era. We already have living proof that America can succeed in the 21st Century. All around us scientists and entrepreneurs are inventing a better future. All around us corporations are re-thinking and re-engineering to produce more, better, and faster, with fewer resources. All around us the private sector and private citizens are changing and adapting to today's competitive realities.

A successful 21st Century America is a Pro-Entrepreneur, Pro-Science, and Technology, Pro-Savings and Investment America that is inventing the best products with the highest values in the world. Second Wave Industries accumulate more and more and get bigger and bigger. Third Wave organizations are subtracting functions instead of adding functions and are subcontracting functions so that they remain quick, efficient and productive.

We need to decentralize some of the power by placing it in the hands of more people. Third Wave organizations are empowered by their employees because these employees often have information and respond to crises and opportunities faster than those on the top. Third Wave organizations want all employees to think, question and take risks — employees who show individualism. Now what we need to do is re-engineer government to follow Third Wave principles by cutting waste, lowering costs, increasing productivity and quality. This will also have the benefit of allowing us to lower taxes on entrepreneurs and investors so we can create more economic growth.

GOVERNMENT IN THE THIRD WAVE

We need to begin this restructuring of government in order to keep up with the rest of the world and the changes in the future. Government should be lean and flexible. It has been my hope ever since I arrived in this body, that Congress and the Executive Branch be more forward-looking institutions. It seems to me that we are always trying to solve yesterday's problems. Instead, as a government, we should be looking at ways to anticipate what lies ahead and enact policies that are future-oriented.

Government structures should be based on Third Wave realities. We should not only down-size government but change what is outdated. Many of the charters for the current cabinet agencies are based on our First Wave or Second Wave principles. We need new departments enabling legislation that would follow Third Wave principles in which government promotes science, trade telecommunications, information and education.

For example, one of the restructuring options which should be considered is the combination of the Departments of Labor and Education. Because of rapidly changing technology we will need to create a system of effective lifetime learning. No longer can one expect that the education one receives in one's youth will be sufficient to enable one to maintain the skill levels necessary to perform optimally in the workplace. That is why a Department of Education and Labor which emphasizes the need for continued lifetime skill improvement will be a necessity for America's competitiveness in a rapidly changing world economy.

Another Executive Branch reform that I have long advocated is the creation of a Department of Science. To me, this would be the focal point for future-oriented programs within the Federal Government. As we enter the 21st Century, science will play an

THIRD WAVE INFORMATION SOCIETY

What is a "Third Wave Information Society"?

The First Wave of change, launched by the agricultural revolution of 10,000 years ago, led to the transition from hunting, gathering and foraging to the great peasant societies of the past. The Second Wave of change, triggered by the industrial revolution some 300 years ago, gave rise to a new factory-centered civilization. It is still spreading in some parts of the world as hundreds of millions of peasants, from Mexico to China, flood into the cities searching for minimal-skill jobs on factory assembly lines.

But even as the Second Wave plays itself out on the global scale, America and other countries are already feeling the impact of a gigantic Third Wave partly based on the substitution of mental power for muscle power in the economy.

The Third Wave is more than just technology and economies. Our transition from a brute force to a brain force economy is accompanied by painful social, cultural, institutional, moral, and political dislocations. The Third Wave helps explain why so many industrial-era institutions, from giant corporations to governments, are dinosaurs gasping for their last breath. It is why America is suffering from simultaneous crises in everything from the education system, the health system, and the family system to the justice system. They were designed to work in a mass industrial society. But America has left that behind.

Driven by global competition and other forces, America today is completing its transition from a Second Wave nation with a rusty smokestack, assembly-line economy to a sleek computer-driven, information and media-dense economy and social system that, surprisingly, will have many features of the pre-industrial past. Swept along by the Third Wave of history, we are creating a new civilization.

Excerpted from the testimony of Alvin and Heidi Toffler before the Joint Economic Committee, June 12, 1995.

increasingly important role as a driver of economic growth. As we have seen in the recent past, inventiveness has been a key to job creation. A Secretary of Science would be the member of the President's Cabinet who would work with the other Cabinet secretaries to assure that new ideas are brought to bear on the policy deliberations of the Executive Branch's most important policy-making council.

The department I am proposing would combine the science elements of the existing Commerce and Energy Departments as those two agencies are terminated. It would also incorporate into the new department the National Aeronautics and Space Administration, the National Science Foundation, the Environmental Protection Agency, as well as the United States Geological Survey. These organizations would no longer be separate independent agencies.

CONCLUSION

For the first time in many years we are looking at a major restructuring of the Executive Branch of government. We should take this opportunity not only to downsize what everyone acknowledges is overly large but also out of date. Many of the charters for the Cabinet agencies were formulated during the 19th century. When the Department of Agriculture was created in 1862, over half the population lived and worked on the family farm. Today's economy is not only based on our agrarian heritage but it is to an increasing extent anchored in science, trade, telecommunications, and information. As we reduce the size of government, we should rationalize what remains into cohesive units which address problems as they exist today.

Economic change can open vast new horizons of growth and employment. Political change can open the doors for more hope and opportunity. Cultural change can create a foundation of values on which to build a future. Technological change can provide the means to pursue our dreams. The challenge we face is to mold those changes in ways that lead to hope rather than hate; foresight rather than fear; virtue rather than victimization; vision rather than vitriol. That challenge is not just for politicians and policy-makers. It is a challenge for all Americans in an era of revolution.

READING

9

EASING THE TAX BURDEN: THE ESSENCE OF PROSPERITY

National Center for Policy Analysis

The National Center for Policy Analysis is a nonprofit, nonpartisan public policy research institute founded in 1983 and internationally known for its studies on public policy issues. It draws on an international network of academic advisors including several Nobel Prize winners, to address the most critical policy issues in the world. Additionally, the NCPA has several policy experts readily available for media inquiries.

The Center concentrates on health care, tax and environmental issues. It is probably best known in the U.S. for its work on tax policy and health policy. The NCPA was founded by John C. Goodman, an economist who serves as its president, and the late Sir Anthony Fisher. Its primary goal is to "discover and promote private alternatives to government regulations and control, solving problems by relying on the strengths of the competitive, entrepreneurial private sector."

■ POINTS TO CONSIDER

1. Contrast Republican claims versus Democratic claims concerning the effect of supply-side tax relief on the economy.

2. Summarize the evidence the article cites in concluding that tax cuts stimulate the economy.

3. Who will receive most of the benefits of the Republican tax proposals? Discuss the factors that support this.

"Are the Republican Tax Cuts Fair?" **National Center for Policy Analysis**, April 3, 1995. Reprinted by permission of the National Center for Policy Analysis, 12655 N. Central Expressway, Suite 720, Dallas, Texas 75243, (214) 386-6272.

One does not have to accept the results of any particular study in order to accept the conclusion that lower taxes can raise national income.

Are the Republican tax cuts fair? The most controversial provisions of the House Republicans' Contract with American are the tax cuts. The question of whether to give parents a $500 child tax credit and, if so, at what income level, is a political decision. But six proposals in the contract are designed specifically to increase economic growth in the United States. These include cutting the capital gains rate in half, indexing capital gains and depreciation expenses and expanding opportunities to contribute to IRA accounts.

Republicans claim that these tax reductions will lead to more jobs, higher wages and a higher standard of living for all. Democratic critics claim that these tax changes are a giveaway to the rich that will have to be funded by higher tax burdens for everyone else.

THE CASE AGAINST THE PROPOSALS

The Democrats' critique is based on two arguments. First, they claim that lowering taxes on investment income does not lead to more overall investment. Therefore, there will be no increase in Gross National Product (GNP). While these policies may alter the way in which the national income pie is divided, they do not affect the total size of the pie, they say.

The critics do not deny that tax policy can change investment decisions. For example, they recognize that a cut in the capital gains tax rate will likely encourage the kinds of investments that generate capital gains and that more liberal rules on IRAs will lead to more IRA deposits. But these investments, they claim, come at the expense of others. On net, the amount of real capital in the economy as a whole will remain the same.

If you buy this argument, you almost have to accept the Democrats' charge that the Republican tax cuts are unfair. If reducing taxes on investment income does not stimulate overall investment, then all it does is shift the tax burden from investors to non-investors. And in our economy, investors disproportionately are high-income people. Among those who earn more than $250,000 a year, for example, 65 percent of income comes from investments.

65

The critics cannot be dismissed lightly. Theirs are the same assumptions used by the Congressional Budget Office and the Joint Committee on Taxation to forecast the effects of proposed legislation. The assumptions also are endorsed by the Clinton Administration's Office of Management and Budget and the U.S. Department of the Treasury.

Yet despite the cachet of the critics, the economic theory they rely on is anything but mainstream. Every President since Franklin D. Roosevelt has believed that the federal government's fiscal policy can affect national income. And — prior to Bill Clinton — every President since John F. Kennedy believed that reducing taxes on investment income can increase total investment and benefit the nation as a whole.

EVIDENCE THAT TAX CUTS SPUR GROWTH

The other side of this argument can be summed up in two words: taxes matter. Proponents of supply-side tax cuts believe that changes in tax rates do not merely shift the tax burden among different taxpayer groups but also can induce people to alter their work effort and their savings and investment plans. These changes cause national income to grow or shrink. Some Democrats claim that this position is voodoo economics, a.k.a. trickle-down economics. Its theoretical underpinnings, they say, were totally discredited during the Reagan administration — witness the mounting federal debt in the 1980s.

In fact, the experience of the 1980s strongly supports the power of tax policy to affect the economy. For example, the liberal Urban Institute concluded that the 23 percent across-the-board reduction in personal income tax rates in the first Reagan term substantially increased labor market participation — especially among marginal workers including teenagers, the elderly and women in two-earner households. Other studies show that throughout the 1980s, investments in equipment and residential and non-residential structures responded to tax rate increases and decreases.

THE RATE OF RETURN ON CAPITAL

Another way to test the validity of the two views is to look at the returns earned by investors. If the capital stock does not change when taxes on investment income change, this implies that the

66

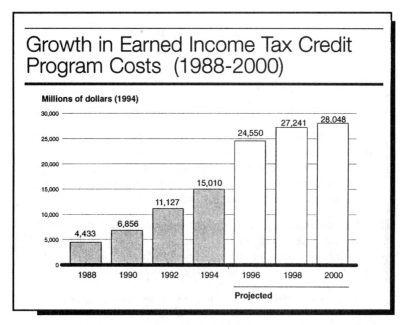

Growth in Earned Income Tax Credit Program Costs (1988-2000)

Millions of dollars (1994)

Year	Value
1988	4,433
1990	6,856
1992	11,127
1994	15,010
1996	24,550
1998	27,241
2000	28,048

Projected

Source: Fiscal year estimates from the Presidents' 1990, 1992, 1994, 1996 budgets.

government can permanently increase or decrease the after-tax rate of return. Does the evidence support this prediction? Hardly.

Gary Robbins and Aldona Robbins, two former U.S. Treasury economists, have calculated the economy-wide after-tax rate of return on capital in the United States over the past 40 years. The figure depicts this calculation, showing that the return on capital tends to be a constant 3.3 percent over time. This finding is consistent with U.S. Department of Commerce measurements of the rate of return earned in manufacturing.

The calculation supports the following conclusion: Not only is the capital stock not fixed, it appears to be infinitely elastic. Specifically, the world capital market appears willing to supply unlimited investment funds to the U.S. economy so long as investors can earn an after-tax average rate of 3.3 percent. In response to a major tax change, the flow of investment funds expands or contracts until the rate of return reaches 3.3 percent. Moreover, the response to a major tax change is relatively quick. Sixty percent takes place within two years, and the full effect is felt within five years.

SOAKING THE RICH

The poverty numbers tell us a great deal about the unin-tended consequences of four years of soak-the-wealthy tax policies under the Bush and Clinton administrations, which have mostly hurt those among lower to middle incomes.

The argument given by the tax-boosters who shoved the top income tax rate up from 28 percent to 31 percent in 1990 was that it would help reduce the deficit and thus improve the economy. But the deficit climbed to nearly $300 billion and the economy went into a recession.

Jobs were cut, payrolls were trimmed and thousands of new enterprises were discouraged from forming as a result of that tax hike, and the people near the bottom as well as the middle class were the ones who suffered most.

Donald Lambro, "Soaking the Rich Creates More Poverty," **Conservative Chronicle**, 26 Oct. 1994: 18.

WHY MOST OF THE BENEFITS GO TO THE NON-RICH

If the after-tax rate of return on capital is constant, then investors will earn roughly the same return regardless of what government does. This implies that the benefits of a larger capital stock tend to go to wage earners rather than owners of capital. Currently, our economy generates $12 in after-tax wages for every $1 of aftertax income to investors. As long as we can give an extra dollar to investors and walk away with $12 in wage income, what difference does it make whether the investors are Wall Street fat cats, Japanese businessmen or little old ladies in tennis shoes? No matter who provides the capital, it's a deal we can't afford to turn down.

Based on the assumption that the rate of return on capital tends to be constant, the Robbinses have forecast that the Republican contract would increase the U.S. economic growth rate by two percentage points and over the next five years, create 3.2 million new jobs, increase the after-tax wage rate by 10.3 percent and produce a total of $3.9 billion in additional after-tax wages.

Other evidence in favor of the power of taxes to spur economic growth comes from a series of studies showing that the overall tax rate significantly affects economic growth. These include studies of the differences in growth rates among nations and among the 50 states as well as studies of the U.S. growth rate over time.

For example, a study by Gerald Scully of the University of Texas at Dallas shows that a total tax rate (federal, state and local) that takes more than 23 percent of gross national product lowers the rate of economic growth in the United States. Had we maintained the 1949 level of 23 percent of GNP instead of allowing the rate to climb to its current 40 percent level, higher growth would have produced twice the national income we currently enjoy. Moreover, at that higher income level, 23 percent of GNP would generate enough tax revenue to pay for all existing federal programs with no federal debt.

One does not have to accept the results of any particular study in order to accept the conclusion that lower taxes can raise national income. Any other conclusion is inconsistent with history, economic evidence and common sense.

TAX CUTS FOR THE FEW: ENDANGERING THE MANY

Walter L. Owensby

The Reverend Walter L. Owensby is a program associate in the Public Policy Office of the Presbyterian Church (USA) in Washington, D.C. He wrote this article for the Stewardship of Public Life, *a quarterly newsletter on social issues published by the Presbyterian Church (USA), 110 Maryland Avenue, N.E., Washington, D.C. 20002, (202) 543-1126.*

■ POINTS TO CONSIDER

1. Summarize the "good ideas" Owensby cites in the House Republican tax bill.

2. Discuss why the author finds the majority of the tax proposals to be inherently unfair.

3. The author refers to the House tax proposals as a replay of "1980s trickle-down economics." Summarize the problems with trickle-down economics according to the author.

4. Contrast the intent of the 1986 tax reform proposals with those of the 104th Congressional session.

Rev. Walter L. Owensby, "House Tax-Cut Bill Favors the Few, Endangers Many," **Stewardship of Public Life, Domestic Poverty and Human Needs,** 2nd Quarter 1995, Presbyterian Church (USA). Reprinted with permission.

After the tax breaks were given, productive invest-ment diminished, job creation did not increase, and the deficit exploded into today's frightening problem.

House Speaker Newt Gingrich regards the "crown jewel" of the Contract with America, a $189 billion tax-cut bill. Politicians normally love cutting taxes since no one likes paying them...The issue is not just whether it is economically wise to give up such massive federal revenues. Also at stake is how fair the proposed cuts are and who will bear the burden of programs slashed or abandoned in order to make reduced taxes possible.

GOOD IDEAS

• There are some positive aspects to the House legislation. The **marriage penalty** is addressed. If a married couple pays more in taxes by filing jointly than if each filed singly, they would receive up to $145 to cover the difference. (Cost in lost federal revenues over five years: $8.5 billion, according to data of the Joint Tax Committee.)

• An **adoption credit** of $5,000 would go to families with annual income below $60,000 to help cover costs of adopting a child. Families with incomes up to $100,000 would receive partial credit. (Cost: $1 billion.)...

• A $500 **elderly care credit** would go to families who care for a disabled parent or grandparent at home. Those whose income is so low that they don't owe taxes would receive a payment from the government. (Cost: $8 billion.)...

The cost in lost revenues of these three good ideas is $17.5 billion. But that leaves the tax-cut bill with $171.5 billion in basically bad ideas.

BAD IDEAS

Some of the tax cuts proposed in the House bill are simply unfair: the vast majority of the benefits go to the few rich and the already comfortable. A Treasury Department analysis shows that less than 16% of the benefits would go to the 60% of families with incomes below $50,000. More than half the advantages are allotted to the top 12% of families whose average income is over $100,000. Of that, the richest 1%, with incomes over $350,000 a year, would receive 20% of the benefits of the whole tax package.

71

When taxes are reduced, the government's revenues go down, and services must be cut to avoid adding to the debt and deficit that is already of such great concern. Most lawmakers backing the tax-cut legislation also profess to support balancing the budget by the year 2002 while protecting spending on the military and Social Security.

The Center on Budget and Policy Priorities estimates that this would require slashing all other federal expenditures (except required interest payments on the national debt) by 30% below what will be needed to maintain current levels of service and commitment. That can only mean massive cuts in domestic programs that mainly benefit moderate-income and low-income families.

Previous House action cuts $66 billion over five years from entitlement programs such as food stamps, school lunches, and welfare. These "savings" are now allocated to paying for the tax cuts that benefit mainly upper-income individuals and families. Billions more will be taken from housing, child care, and job training programs.

TAX CUTS

Here are some of the specific tax cuts for individuals in the House bill that are bad ideas.

A **family tax credit** would allow families earning up to $200,000 to take $500 off their taxes for each child under 18. (Cost: $105 billion.) Given the rising cost of rearing children, that sounds useful and egalitarian. Unfortunately, the credit as passed by the House is not refundable; that is, it is not returned in cash to families too poor to pay income tax. What this means is that those who need the help most are left out. Far better would be to limit the benefit to families in the bottom half of the income scale.

A new version of **individual retirement accounts (IRAs)** would allow all workers and non-working spouses to contribute up to $2,000 each to retirement funds where earnings would not be taxed upon withdrawal. (Costs unspecified billions in the long-run.) This bill does not simply defer taxes until retirement when most persons drop into a lower tax bracket. It eliminates all taxation on interest and asset growth. While this would theoretically be available to all, it will benefit only those families that can save

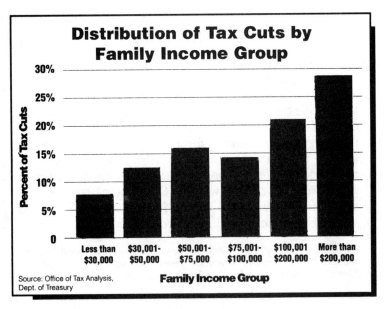

Distribution of Tax Cuts by Family Income Group

Source: Office of Tax Analysis,
Dept. of Treasury

Source: Office of Tax Analysis, Dept. of the Treasury

$2,000 to $4,000 in a year. That is beyond the means of perhaps one-quarter to one-third of the population. In fact, studies suggest that 95% of the benefits would go the fifth of families with the highest income.

Capital gains taxes would be restructured to give extraordinary advantages to investors. (Cost: $32 billion.) As a first benefit, there would be no taxes on half of a person's capital gains earnings. The result would be to reduce the top effective tax rate to just 19.8%. In addition, no taxes would be paid on increased asset value due to inflation. There is an argument for such indexation, but it is not applied in most other parts of the tax structure, so why here?

The House bill reduces the percentage of **Social Security** earnings subject to taxation from 85% to just 50% for families with incomes of $44,000 or individuals who earn $34,000. And persons age 65 to 69 would be able to earn up to $30,000 before beginning to lose benefits. That rises from the current $11,280. To those near the age, this sounds good. But can the nation afford the $23 billion price tag in lost revenues?

The new law on **estate and gift taxes** would raise the amount that is excluded from taxation from $600,000 to $750,000. (Cost:

TAX-CUTTING REGIME

The Reagan-Bush duo, 1981-92, has claimed to be a conservative, tax-cutting, anti-spending, budget-balancing regime. But after 11 years, most Americans are paying more taxes while the corporations and the rich pay less — a trillion dollars less in the 80s. Civilian spending may be checked, but another trillion dollars for a needless military escalation went to the Pentagon in the 80s. The result of all this has been a quadrupling of the national debt by the Reagan-Bush White House in concert with the Democratic Congress. All of this is still going on, with a $400 billion deficit to be added this year to a $4 trillion national debt.

Excerpted from a review of William Greider's book, **Who Will Tell the People: The Betrayal of American Democracy**. By George McGovern, "Democracy in Danger," **In These Times,** 6-12 May, 1992: 13.

$6.8 billion.) While it can be argued that some productive assets like farm land passing to family members should go untaxed, simply foregoing revenues on general estates up to three-quarters of a million dollars seems excessive.

The House-passed tax-cut bill also provides broad new benefits to corporations. High-income individuals and families will be the primary beneficiaries since they are the largest investors. The top **corporate capital gains** rate would be reduced from 35% to 25%, and as for individual investors, the amount taxed would be discounted for inflation.

Businesses would also benefit from far more liberal **depreciation** rules. The present system allows companies to write off the full purchase price of buildings and equipment. The new legislation would index the value of assets for inflation and actually allow a firm to reduce its tax bill by more than the original purchase price — in some cases even double.

The grand prize for business, however, is the repeal of the **alternative minimum tax.** Originally proposed by President Reagan, it was adopted in 1986 to prevent profitable corporations from avoiding taxes by amassing tax write-offs for otherwise unproductive investments. Large and profitable companies now pay at least something in taxes. The House-passed bill would eliminate that and return to the time when creative bookkeeping rather than business acumen determined total profitability. (Cost: $17 billion.) That may be good for the balance sheet, but it undercuts the logic of free enterprise and unfairly shifts the tax burden.

REFORM INTENT

The intent of the 1986 tax reform was to simplify the tax code by reducing the basic rates of taxation in exchange for closing personal and business tax loopholes. The House bill continues to drive down the rates, but the loopholes are back with a vengeance...In other words, this tax-cut bill is a replay of the trickle-down economics of the 1980s. The problem is that it didn't work. After the tax breaks were given, productive investment diminished, job creation did not increase, and the deficit exploded into today's frightening problem.

THE LAND OF OPPORTUNITY

Newt Gingrich

Newt Gingrich represents the 6th Congressional District of Georgia. He was elected Speaker of the House of Representatives for the 104th Congressional session, the first Republican majority session in forty years.

■ POINTS TO CONSIDER

1. Discuss the significance of the Contract with America for Speaker Gingrich.

2. Summarize and explain several government reforms necessary in order to create Gingrich's "opportunity society."

3. Describe the role of technology in enhancing opportunity.

4. Discuss the effect that the deficit and national debt will have for the economy in the future.

Newt Gingrich, "The Contract with America: A Report on the New Congress," **Vital Speeches**, 1 May 1995: 423-6. Reprinted by permission of **Vital Speeches**.

We are determined to remake this government until every child knows that he or she has all the opportunities of an American.

The House Republicans have signed a Contract with America. We signed this contract and made some promises to you and to ourselves. You elected us and we have been keeping our word. With your help we're bringing about real change. We made Congress subject to the same laws as everyone else, we cut congressional committee staffs and budgets by 30%, and we voted on every item in the Contract. And I can tell you tonight we are going to sell one Congressional building and privatize a Congressional parking lot.

While we've done a lot, this contract has never been about curing all the ills of the nation. One hundred days cannot overturn the neglect of decades. The contract's purpose has been to show that change is possible, that even in Washington you can do what you say you're going to do. In short, we've wanted to prove to you that democracy still has the vitality and the will to do something about the problems facing our nation. And it seems to me, whether you are conservative or liberal, that is a very positive thing...The big battles will deal with how we remake the Government of the United States. The measure of everything we do will be whether we are creating a better future with more opportunities for our children...

WELFARE

A truly compassionate government would replace the welfare state with opportunity. The welfare system's greatest cost is the human cost to the poor. In the name of "compassion" we have funded a system that is cruel and destroys families. Its failure is reflected by the violence, brutality, child abuse and drug addiction in every local TV news broadcast.

Poor Americans are trapped in unsafe government housing, saddled with rules that are anti-work, anti-family and anti-property. Let me give you some statistics on this failure. Welfare spending now exceeds $300 billion a year. Yet despite all the trillions that have been spent since 1970, the number of children in poverty has increased 40%. You may have noticed that welfare spending goes up, and so does the number of children born outside marriage. Year by year they track each other. The more tax money we spend on welfare, the more children who are born without benefit of family and without strong bonds of love and nurturing. If money alone were the answer, this would be a paradise.

Since money is not the answer, it should be clear we have a moral imperative to remake the welfare system so every American can lead a full life. After all, we believe that all men and women are endowed by our Creator with certain unalienable rights, among which are life, liberty and the pursuit of happiness. We are determined to remake this government until every child of every racial background, in every neighborhood in America, knows that he or she has all the opportunities of an American.

OPPORTUNITY

I believe we have to do a number of things to become an opportunity society. We must restore freedom by ending bureaucratic micromanagement here in Washington. As any good business leader will tell you, decisions should be made as closely as possible to the source of the problem. This country is too big and too diverse for Washington to have the knowledge to make the right decision on local matters; we've got to return power back to you — to your families, your neighborhoods, your local and state governments. We need to promote economic growth by reducing regulation, taxation and frivolous lawsuits. Everywhere I go Americans complain about an overly complicated tax code and an arrogant, unpredictable and unfair Internal Revenue Service. This summer we will begin hearings on bold, decisive reform of the income tax system. We're looking at a simplified flat tax and other ways to bring some sense to the disorder and inequity of our tax system.

Another reason for optimism is the tremendous opportunities being created by the information technologies. Tremendous is a big word so let me show you an example. This is a traditional telephone cable. This is a fiber optic cable. You can barely see it. This almost invisible fiber optic cable is equal to 64 of these big bulky traditional cables. Now that is a tremendous opportunity. With these breakthroughs the most rural parts of America can be connected electronically to the best learning, the best health care and the best work opportunities in the world. Distance learning can offer new hope to the present inner city neighborhood, the poorest Indian reservation and the smallest rural community. Distance medicine can bring the best specialist in the world to your health clinic, your hospital.

Business Investment Has Surged

Percent

Real Business Investment in Equipment as a Percent of GDP

Source: Senate Finance Committee, February 8, 1995.

Furthermore, the breakthroughs in molecular medicine may cure Alzheimer's, eliminate many genetic defects and offer new cures for diabetes, cancer and heart disease. These breakthroughs combined with preventive care and medical innovations can create better health for all Americans. And we will pass a reform so that when you change jobs you can't be denied insurance even if you or your family have health problems.

We will improve Medicare by offering a series of new Medicare options that will increase senior citizens control over their own health care and guarantee them access to the best and most modern systems of health research and health innovation. My father, my mother, and my mother-in-law all rely on Medicare. I know how crucial the Medicare system is to senior Americans, and we will insure that it continues to provide the care our seniors need with more choices at less cost to the elderly.

All around us opportunities for a better life are being developed but our government all too often ignores or even blocks them. We need those breakthroughs which create new jobs, new health, and new learning, to give us the opportunity and growth to deal with our budgetary problems. We must get our national finances in order. The time has come to balance the federal budget and to free our children from the burdens upon their prosperity and their lives.

NATIONAL DEBT

This is a Congressional voting card. This card goes into a box on the House floor and the computer records the member's vote. The Congressional voting card is the most expensive credit card in the world. For two generations it has been used to pile up trillions in debt that our children and grandchildren will eventually have to repay.

Now a big debt has a big impact. To make such numbers real, let me give you an example. If you have a child or grandchild born this year, that child is going to pay $187,000 in taxes in his lifetime to pay his share of the interest on the debt. Yes, you heard me right, $187,000 in taxes, in his lifetime — that's over $3,500 in taxes every year of his working life just to pay interest on the debt we are leaving him. That's before he is taxed to pay for Social Security or Medicare, education or highways or police or the national defense. You know and I know, that's just not fair.

It was once an American tradition to pay off the mortgage and leave the children the farm. Now we seem to be selling the farm and leaving our children the mortgage.

BALANCED BUDGET

Our goals are simple. We don't want our children to drown in debt. We want baby boomers to be able to retire with the same security as their parents. We want our senior Americans to be able to rely on Medicare without fear. These are the reasons why, as Franklin Delano Roosevelt said, "Our generation has a rendezvous with destiny." This is the year we rendezvous with our destiny to establish a clear plan to balance the budget. It can no longer be put off. That is why I am speaking to you so frankly.

The budget can be balanced even with the problems of the federal government. It can be balanced without touching a penny of Social Security and without raising taxes. In fact, spending overall can go up every year. We simply must limit annual spending increases to about 3% between now and 2002. The key is the willingness to change, to set priorities, to redesign the government, to recognize that this is not the 1960s or '70s but the 1990s and we need a government to match the times. As I've said, Social Security is off the table. But that leaves a lot on the table — corporate welfare, subsidies of every special interest. Defense is on the table. I'm a hawk, but a cheap hawk.

As the budget battle rages over the coming months, you will hear screams from the special interest groups. I'm sure you've already heard the dire cries that we are going to take food out of the mouths of school children, that we are going to feed them ketchup. The fact of the matter is that all we did was vote to increase school lunch money four and a half percent every year for five years and give the money to the states to spend, because we thought they would do a better job than the federal government of ensuring that the children's meals were nutritional...

POSSIBILITIES

Whatever the arguments, this remains a country of unparalleled possibilities. We as a people have the natural ability to respond to change. That is what we do best when the government is not in the way. Our potential is as great and prosperous as it's ever been in our history. From now on all roads lead forward...If I had one message for this country on this day when we celebrate the act of keeping our word, it would be a simple message: Idealism is American. To be romantic is American. It's okay to be a skeptic, but don't be a cynic. It's okay to raise good questions, but don't assume the worst. It's okay to report difficulties, but it's equally good to report victories...

I am here to say that we're going to open a dialogue, because we want to create a new partnership with the American people, a plan to remake the government and balance the budget, which is the American people's plan — not the House Republican plan, not the Gingrich plan, but the plan of the American people. And it is in that spirit of committing ourselves idealistically, committing ourselves romantically, believing in America, that we celebrate having kept our word. And we promise to begin a new partnership, so that together we and the American people can give our children and our country a new birth of freedom.

READING

12

THE LAND OF INEQUALITY

David Beckmann

David Beckmann is director of Bread for the World, *a non-profit, Christian, ecumenical organization that seeks justice for the world's hungry. Its headquarters are in Silver Springs, Maryland.*

■ **POINTS TO CONSIDER**

1. Describe the possible effects of government cut-backs in the 1980s for lower income people.

2. Discuss the possible effects of budget cutting in domestic social welfare and foreign sustainable development programs.

3. Does the author feel confident that private charity and religious institutions can replace the federal government after social welfare spending cuts? Why or why not?

4. Why does Beckmann depict America as a land of inequality?

David Beckmann, "Assault on the Poor," **The Christian Century**, 5 April 1995: 356-8. Copyright 1995 Christian Century Foundation. Reprinted by permission from the April 5, 1995 issue of **The Christian Century**.

Those who favor reducing assistance to the poor should stop pretending that by slashing benefits to the needy they are actually acting in the best interests of the poor.

Congress is waging war on poor people. Domestic programs that help low-income Americans, as well as international programs that help poor people overseas, are under attack. The House of Representatives voted 234-199 to approve the so-called Personal Responsibility Act, which would cut $66 billion from food and other domestic anti-poverty programs over five years; at least $26 billion is scheduled to be axed from food programs alone. The act would also transfer to block grants many anti-poverty programs, shifting responsibility to the states and eliminating many entitlements and federal standards.

Cutting $66 billion in public spending will fall far short of making up for the $189 billion in tax breaks over five years that Republicans have crafted for upper- and middle-income people. Where the odd $100 billion in lost revenues will come from is anyone's guess. One thing, though, is clear. For the 39 million Americans who subsist below the poverty line (set at less than $15,000 a year for a family of four), $66 billion in cuts would take away an average of $1,700 per person. Senate and Presidential actions are expected to moderate House proposals, but poor people are certainly going to turn out to be the big losers of last November's elections.

CHURCHES

Some say that churches and charities can provide the services that government is abandoning. But $66 billion is more than the total annual revenues of all religious communities in the country. If the country's 350,000 churches would try to make up for the shortfall, each would have to come up with an additional $190,000. To be sure, churches, especially those in low-income communities, have already responded to growing poverty and hunger in our country. Independent Sector, which studies charitable giving, estimates that religious communities' aid to the needy soared from $1 billion in 1986 to $7 billion in 1991, while their total revenue dropped from $50 billion to $48 billion.

PRIVATE FEEDING

Fifteen years ago this country didn't have many soup kitchen or food banks, but churches and other concerned people responded to government cutbacks and growing hunger in the 1980s with a massive movement of private feeding. Now 150,000 private agencies provide some $3 to $4 billion in groceries each year for hungry Americans. Yet the private feeding movement hasn't kept up with the number of hungry people. And if the Personal Responsibility Act passes, funding for food stamps, school meals and other child nutrition programs will drop by more than $4 billion from this year to next. The decline in funding would cancel out what millions of donors and volunteers achieve.

SAFETY NET

Attempts by our political leaders to make churches and charities the social safety net for the nation have only succeeded in hindering these institutions from doing what they do best. Churches are good at helping people in need take responsibility for their actions. Some House Republicans claim that cutting or ending financial benefits will encourage personal responsibility among low-income people. But reduced benefits won't be as effective in discouraging teen pregnancy as churches can be.

To cite another example, nonprofit social services are probably more effective than government agencies in helping low-income people with drug and alcohol problems. But churches and charities have been forced to spend more and more of their time and effort just feeding hungry people. At the very least those who favor reducing assistance to the poor should stop pretending that by slashing benefits to the needy they are actually acting in the best interests of the poor.

The Bible teaches that people do indeed bear a responsibility for supporting themselves. "The person who will not work shall not eat," the New Testament says. That's the early Christian community's version of the Personal Responsibility Act. The Bible also teaches that individuals have a responsibility to people in need: that biblical message has fueled the private feeding movement of the past 15 years.

However, the Bible also teaches that poverty is a social responsibility. The prophets preached about social justice especially to Israel and Judea's kings, the governmental authority of their day.

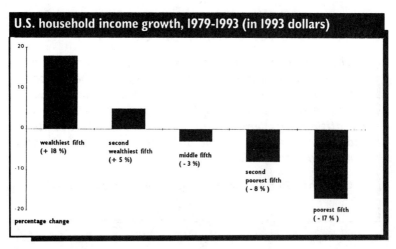

U.S. household income growth, 1979-1993 (in 1993 dollars)

wealthiest fifth
(+ 18 %)

second
wealthiest fifth
(+ 5 %)

middle fifth
(- 3 %)

second
poorest fifth
(- 8 %)

poorest fifth
(- 17 %)

percentage change

Source: The Democratic Socialists of America

If U.S. church leaders have been echoing the prophets, not enough churchgoing voters, nor government authorities, have been convinced.

WAR AGAINST THE POOR

The war against the poor is being waged internationally as well, but this campaign isn't stirring much controversy. The TV cameras are no longer focused on Goma, Zaire, where millions fled last summer from Rwanda. The camps that sheltered tens of thousands of orphaned children are being shut down, and Newt Gingrich is not proposing orphanages for them. Nor is he proposing more classrooms for children in Africa's emerging democracies, such as South Africa, Mali and Benin.

Foreign-aid spending accounts for less than one percent of our federal budget. Each U.S. family spends just $3 annually on assistance to Africa. Yet the committee chairs who handle foreign aid in this Congress intend to slash assistance and to reorient what's left even more toward U.S. commercial and political interests. They are proposing cuts of some $2.5 billion from the $13.7 billion foreign-aid budget, with the heaviest cuts coming in the area of development assistance...

SUPPORTING THE POOR

The cold war competition was the main engine of foreign aid.

OVERCLASS AND OPPORTUNITY

The American oligarchy spares no pains in promoting the belief that it does not exist...Amounting, with their dependents, to about 20 percent of the population, this relatively new and still evolving political and social oligarchy is not identified with any particular region of the country. Homogeneous and nomadic, the overclass is the first truly national upper class in American history...

Michael Lind, "To Have and Have Not," **Harper's Magazine**, June 1995: 36, 37.

Since the end of the cold war, leaders of both political parties have become markedly less interested in poorer parts of the world. Religious groups, environment and population groups and, increasingly, private voluntary organizations that work overseas are now the main advocates for aid that supports sustainable development and poverty reduction. In Washington today the churches' most profoundly countercultural message is its concern about world hunger. How can concerned people of faith respond to today's war on the poor?

- Write to your representatives and, especially, senators, telling them you want them to save development assistance to Africa, the federal food programs and assistance to poor people generally.

- Join Bread for the World or some other network that keeps you apprised of current political developments that affect poor and hungry people. This year, about 1,000 churches across the country are taking up an "offering of letters" to save development aid to Africa.

- Give money and time to political candidates who care.

These methods of active citizenship do work. We also need to develop prudent strategies. Churches and charities that mobilize food assistance must also help the people they feed register to vote. The many organizations dedicated to helping poor people, both domestically and internationally, must rethink how we can together actually reduce hunger and poverty over the longterm. In the process, charities will become more political.

We also need to think creatively about reforming public assistance programs. We should push to reform domestic poverty programs in ways that will help employable people move up and out of poverty. Real welfare reform will cost more money, not less, but it will pay off for taxpayers and everyone else in the long term. We should also work for foreign-aid reform — for a shift of funding toward programs that improve the livelihood of poor people and protect the environment. We certainly don't want to defend foreign aid as it was shaped by the cold war.

READING

13

A BALANCED BUDGET AMENDMENT: THE POINT

U.S. House Committee on the Budget

The House Budget Committee is chaired by John Kasich, a Republican representing the 12th Congressional District of Ohio. Kasich is one of the leading conservative voices in the House of Representatives. The following is excerpted from a committee report representing the majority view of the committee.

■ POINTS TO CONSIDER

1. Discuss what the reading cites as the reasons for the large national debt.

2. Analyze the effect of persistent deficit spending on the tax-payer.

3. Explain the concept of "intergenerational equity."

4. Beyond the moral argument against "borrowing from the future," discuss the present and future arguments against deficit expenditure.

5. Discuss the reasons Congressional deficit reduction efforts in the past failed.

Excerpted from a House Budget Committee print on the balanced budget amendment, **It's Not the Money, It's the Principle**, House Budget Committee, Washington, D.C.: U.S. Government Printing Office, Jan. 1995.

A balanced budget is a clear and positive goal. It simply measures whether total government spending matches total government revenues.

The most important point in the debate is whether a balanced budget norm should be an irrevocable part of the Nation's basic, and permanent, political framework. The annual spending decisions needed to reach balance from today's deficit levels are important, but not primary. This confusion reflects the critics' misunderstanding of the Constitution as a governing document. Even more important than the amendment's value as a budget enforcement tool is its potential role in maintaining a stable, responsible Federal Government.

THE AMENDMENT AS A PRINCIPLE OF GOVERNING

The first and most important issue in debating a balanced budget amendment is whether the practice of balancing spending and revenues should be treated as a fundamental principle of governing.

In its simplest form, a balanced budget would require policy makers to hold the total level of spending to the amount of revenue available each year. Embracing this practice in the Constitution would mean that balancing revenues and spending should be a fundamental condition of governing, just as are the separation of powers and the means of electing representatives. It also would restore a sense among taxpayers about the relationship between the government services they receive and the level of taxes they pay. Without this balance, it is impossible for the taxpayers to judge the tradeoffs between one government program and another, or between spending and taxes in general. It is also impossible for policymakers to judge the public's true priorities because the financing of government programs overall is not clearly related to their cost.

For most of the Nation's history, balancing budgets was assumed as a normal operation procedure. Whether this practice should be restored as a permanent condition for governing is the most important aspect of the balanced budget amendment debate. Until 1962, administrations and Congresses adhered to budget policies based on an uncomplicated but deeply rooted tradition: "a taboo against budget deficits." Congresses and administrations simply accepted that balancing the budget should be the norm. This was far more than a budgetary or economic matter. The practice reflected a sense of balance in political relationships, between political cultures, and among social orders. As Harry S. Truman put it: "There is nothing sacred about the pay-as-you-go idea so far as I am concerned except that it represents the soundest principle of financing that I know." No doubt this commonsense attitude is one reason why 80 percent of the American public favors a balanced budget amendment, even as many technicians and policymakers in Washington attempt to dismiss it.

The practice of balancing budgets was not tied to any particular statute or written constitutional provision. But it did reflect what Nobel Laureate James M. Buchanan has termed "our effective constitution," and amounted to a moral imperative. It was "universally considered immoral" to spend beyond the government's means, except in periods of emergency.

The balanced budget imperative was reflected by the government's practices after major wars. In 1943, in the midst of World War II, the Federal deficit soared to 31.1 percent of Gross Domestic Product (GDP). But within two years after the war, the budget was balanced and in 1948 the government ran a surplus of $11.8 billion. During the Korean war, the government's deficit reached 1.8 percent of GDP; but once again, the budget was balanced by 1956, shortly after the war's end.

The moral imperative began to break down in 1962, when President Kennedy — in a speech at Yale — endorsed the Keynesian view that deficit spending could be used to manipulate the economy. But it was not until 1974 — when President Johnson's Great Society programs were reaching fruition and Congress was "reforming" its budget process, that the long-term, chronic deficit problem took hold. Unlike the previous postwar periods, the government could not balance its budget after Vietnam, and by 1976 the deficit had reached 4.4 percent of GDP.

A SENSE OF ORDER

Balanced budgets reflect a sense of order in the government's business, while deficit spending year after year promotes a nagging sense of disorder. The effect can be traced to the experience of the individual taxpayer. Because the levels of government ser-

POPULAR SUPPORT

Public opinion polls have long indicated more than 75 percent support for a balanced budget amendment. The legislatures of more than 30 states have endorsed a resolution requesting Congress to approve a balanced budget/tax limitation amendment and authorizing a constitutional convention to draft such an amendment if Congress fails to act. More than two-thirds of the Senate approved a proposed amendment with strong provisions on federal deficits, taxes, and new uncompensated mandates in 1982. A similar amendment with a stronger balanced budget rule, a weaker tax rule, and no mandate provision failed to pass the House by only seven votes in 1990.

Excerpted from the testimony of William A. Niskanen, Chairman, **The Cato Institute**, before The House Judiciary Committee, January 9, 1995.

vices and taxation are persistently out of balance, so is the taxpayer's fundamental experience of government. Taxpayers are likely to feel — correctly — that the government itself is out of control. Indeed, chronic deficit spending suggests that the government has grown beyond the level ratified by the taxpayers. This effect is clearly related to the general dissatisfaction with government that voters have expressed.

The absence of a balanced budget norm also makes it impossible for elected representatives to govern properly. When taxpayers' experience of government is out of balance, as described above — and when taxpayers have grown accustomed to receiving more public goods than they pay for — politicians cannot measure the public's true spending priorities because there is no assumed limit on the amount of available resources. Policymakers cannot determine whether the public really is willing to pay more taxes for a specific service — or to give up some government services for the sake of lower taxes — because the two are chronically unrelated. Restoring a balance between spending and taxes would force choices from among the various public services that the government provides. Without such a balance, the question of choices and priorities is moot, and proper governing becomes impossible.

91

THE EFFECT ON FUTURE GENERATIONS

The most frequently cited moral case against deficit spending concerns "intergenerational equity." According to this argument, the borrowing needed to finance current Federal deficits will have to be serviced by taxpayers in the future. Most of these future tax-payers are currently unrepresented; they have no say in the taxing and spending decisions of the present, and they gain no direct benefit from the consumption that current deficits are financing. This is yet another moral reason why deficit financing must be curtailed.

This practice of "borrowing from the future" affects more than government taxing and spending policies. It also depresses the potential for future economic growth and future standards of living. As a result, the taxpayers of the future are being obligated to finance current deficit spending in two ways: through the taxes that will be required to service the debt, and through the poten-tially sacrificed gains in their standards of living. These taxpayers are unrepresented in the current decision-making process.

This deficit financing is not in response to unusual economic distress; it has persisted and grown in good times and bad. Nor does it answer any national emergency, such as a war, in which borrowing from the future might be justified to ensure that a decent future will occur. The principal source of today's spending growth is in domestic programs — mainly entitlements — that have been expanded and augmented over a period of decades. The chronic borrowing used to finance this spending growth entails draining the Nation's investment pool for the sake of pre-sent-day consumption. Even government domestic programs described as investments in human capital — education and health care often are defined this way — involve substantial amounts of present-day consumption. To the extent that this con-sumption is financed by borrowing, the result is, in fact, a reversal of investment: Instead of husbanding today's resources so they can be used in the future, the current practice lays claim on the future's resources so they can be spent today.

THE AMENDMENT AS AN ENFORCEMENT TOOL

The discussion above explains why balancing budgets is neces-sary for proper governing — and why the requirement, therefore, warrants treatment in the Nation's Constitution. The need for a solid, budgetary enforcement tool is unmistakable. History shows that past deficit reduction efforts have been too weak to achieve their goals. Three times in the past 10 years, Congress has sought to tame deficits by legislative means. All three attempts have failed. The first of these was the Gramm-Rudman-Hollings deficit-reduction act. This measure imposed automatic spending cuts, called sequesters, if Congress failed to meet specific, declining, deficit targets each year. Adherence to the law broke down in 1990 in the face of a potential $40-billion sequester in fiscal year 1991.

Gramm-Rudman-Hollings was supplanted by the 1990 budget agreement, which called for $500 billion in deficit reduction over five years, including $158 billion in higher taxes. By 1993, it appeared deficits were still growing. So the Democrat majorities in the House and Senate passed — and President Clinton signed — the Omnibus Budget Reconciliation Act of 1993. This bill, containing $240 billion in higher taxes, was supposed to trim deficits by another $500 billion over five years. Yet Congressional Budget Office projections show that after a slight dip, predicted even before enactment of OBRA 1993, deficits will begin to trend upward again, and will continue to grow indefinitely.

CONCLUSION

Ultimately, the critics of a balanced budget amendment fear that such an amendment would curtail their ability to maintain the *status quo* of the Federal Government. Continuing deficits also gives them an excuse to continue raising taxes. Those who support the amendment can best do so by rejecting the distracting efforts of the critics and restoring the fundamental terms of the debate:

• That balanced budgets are an appropriate and necessary condition for proper governing.

• That Congress needs an ironclad enforcement tool to reach a balanced budget.

• That a balanced budget commitment is needed for the long term, so that Congress will continue its efforts at restraining spending until the job is done.

A BALANCED BUDGET AMENDMENT: THE COUNTERPOINT

Paul Wellstone

Senator Paul Wellstone is a Democrat representing the State of Minnesota. He is one of the leading progressive voices in the U.S. Senate. Formerly, Wellstone was a professor of political science at Carleton College in Northfield, Minnesota.

■ POINTS TO CONSIDER

1. Evaluate the potential effect of a balanced budget amendment in a time of economic recession or depression.

2. Contrast operational spending with investment spending. What example does Wellstone cite to explain the difference?

3. Assess the role of the Social Security System in a balanced budget amendment debate.

4. Discuss what Wellstone cites as the reason for the size of the national debt.

5. Summarize the reasons why upper income Americans will benefit from the passage of a balanced budget amendment. Contrast this with its effect on middle and working class Americans.

Excerpted from comments by Senator Paul Wellstone (D-MN) on the Senate floor, March 2, 1995.

We cannot give over our budget-balancing responsibilities to a machine, a mechanism. That responsibility is ours.

As I have consistently argued, in my judgment we do not need to amend the U.S. Constitution to balance the Federal budget. Instead, we must continue to make tough choices on actual legislative proposals, as I have done, to cut wasteful and unnecessary post-cold war defense spending, to continue to reduce low priority domestic spending, to completely restructure the way we finance and deliver health care in this country — in both the public and private sector — and to scale back special tax breaks for very wealthy interests in our society who have for a long time not been required to pay their fair share. That approach is the only responsible, fair way to bring our annual Federal deficits, and the much larger Federal debt, under control.

For the last 15 years or so, that is what the Congress has been unwilling to do, and that is the source of a lot of frustration in the country. Congress has been unable to muster and sustain a majority to make difficult budget choices. We have seen illustrated here in the Senate over and over again a central problem: The political gap between the promise to cut spending, and actual follow-through on that promise. I make this point because I want to underscore that many of those who have been beating their chests the hardest about a balanced budget amendment have often been among those who have consistently voted against these actual deficit reduction proposals. We cannot give over our budget-balancing responsibilities to a machine, a mechanism. That responsibility is ours. Of course, I support balancing the Federal budget in a responsible, fair way. Despite all of the rhetoric today, we all at least agree on that basic goal.

In recent years, the borrow-and-spend policies of the 1980s and early 1990s have come home to roost, rekindling public support for drastic measures. But just so that we don't lose our historical perspective in this debate, I think it's important to recognize that the problem of huge Federal budget deficits is a relatively recent one, going back only to the early 1980s. It's just not true, as some amendment proponents imply, that the Federal Government has been spending way beyond its means for decades.

The Reagan and Bush administrations gave America by far its 10 largest budget deficits in our history. The huge tax cuts and large defense increases of that era are still costing us. Whatever your party affiliation or perspective on enacting this amendment, that is indisputable. If it were not for the interest costs on the debt accumulated during the 1981-92 period, the Federal budget would be in balance in 1996 and headed toward surplus thereafter.

I am not trying to explain away large deficits over the last decade or so, but simply to point out that they are, more than anything else, a direct result of the misguided and now thoroughly discredited fiscal policy called supply-side economics. Despite the urgings of some of our colleagues in the new House leadership, and some of the provisions of the Republican Contract for America, we must not turn down that supply-side road again.

Opposing the amendment has not been easy, or politically popular. But since I have spoken several times on various amendments that have been proposed over the course of the last few weeks, let me try to summarize one last time my major reasons for voting against this amendment.

POTENTIAL DISASTERS

Consider the potential risk that the spending cuts required by the amendment could push a soft economy into a recession, or in a worse case, deepen an existing recession and push us into a depression. Now when the economy slips into recession, Federal spending helps to cushion the fall by increasing unemployment insurance and other assistance programs for low- and moderate-income people. At the same time, income tax collections drop because people and businesses are making less money in a recession.

But under the amendment, Congress would be forced, perversely, to do the opposite: raise taxes, cut spending, and push the economy into an economic freefall. The so-called automatic economic stabilizers like unemployment insurance that have proven so useful in recent decades would be gone, and we would instead effectively enshrine in the constitution the economic policies of Herbert Hoover. With fiscal policy enjoined by the amendment, sole responsibility for stabilizing the economy would rest with the Federal Reserve. And with their almost exclusive focus on fighting inflation these days, more often than not they end up protecting Wall Street investors — not average working families.

96

NOT ALL EXPENDITURE IS THE SAME

Most Americans believe that a balanced budget, like a balanced checkbook, is a good idea. They argue that America, like a family, should always balance its budget. But this overlooks a key fact: The household budgets of most middle class Americans have substantial debt, either for a car, a home, or a college education for their kids.

This reflects a central problem with the amendment. It ignores the difference between two different types of spending: investments for the future, and "operating," or day-to-day, spending. Taking out a mortgage on a home is investing in your family's future; taking one out to pay for next year's vacation is not. This is acknowledged by most State governments, many of whom are required to balance their operating budgets — but not their investment budgets. American business agrees; incurring debt to invest and expand a business has long been a hallmark of business strategies for sustained growth.

This balanced budget amendment also fails to protect the Social Security trust funds from being raided to balance the Federal budget. Despite the promises of the proponents that they will not balance the budget on the backs of Social Security recipients, they have refused to explicitly protect this program in the language of the constitutional amendment itself. In fact, they fought hard to defeat our Social Security amendment. That is as good an indication of their future intentions regarding Social Security as anything we have seen.

TAX BURDEN SHIFTED

There is another problem with this constitutional amendment. For many in Minnesota, it will likely mean an increase in personal income, sales, and property taxes needed to offset the loss in federal aid from crime control to higher education, roads and bridges to farm programs, rural economic development to Medicare. This shell game, in which costs are simply shifted from the Federal Government onto the States, would force Minnesota to fund these efforts on its own. A recent Treasury Department study concluded that an increase of between 9 and 13 percent in Minnesota taxes would be required to make up the difference. In reality, a vote for the balanced budget amendment is really a vote for a trickle-down tax increase.

97

EFFORTS TO SCRUTINIZE TAX BREAKS FOR WEALTHY BLOCKED

While the constitutional amendment's proponents don't seem to mind that it could require states to raise state taxes by large margins, they are adamantly opposed to making sure that wealthy corporations and others pay their fair share of the deficit reduction burden.

It is a fact, often overlooked, that we can spend money just as easily through the Tax Code, through what are called "tax expenditures," as we can through the normal appropriations process. Spending is spending, whether it comes in the form of a government check or in the form of a tax break for some special purpose, like a subsidy, a credit, a deduction, or accelerated depreciation for this type of investment or that. These tax expenditures — in some cases they are tax loopholes — allow some taxpayers to escape paying their fair share, and thus make everyone else pay at higher rates. These arcane tax breaks are simply special exceptions to the normal rules, rules that oblige all of us to share the burdens of citizenship by paying our taxes.

The Congressional Joint Tax Committee has estimated that tax expenditures cost the U.S. Treasury over $420 billion every single year. And they estimate that if we don't hold them in check, that amount will grow by $60 billion to over $485 billion by 1999. Now some tax expenditures serve important public purposes, like supporting charitable organizations, and should be retained. But many of these must be on the table along with other spending as we look for places to cut the deficit. I could not find any hint of interest in cutting corporate tax breaks in the Republican contract. I think this is because many of the benefits of these tax breaks go to very high-income people with wealth and power and clout in our society, and to corporations with high-powered lobbyists. They're the ones for whom the contract provides an estimated $169 billion windfall that would resurrect the tax-shelter industry and effectively slash corporate rates.

At a time when we are talking about potentially huge spending cuts in meat inspections designed to insure against outbreaks of disease; or in higher education aid for middle class families; or in protection for our air, our lakes, and our land; or in highways; or in community development programs for states and localities; or in sewer and water projects for our big cities; or in safety net programs for vulnerable children, we should be willing to weigh these cuts against special tax loopholes on which we spend billions each year. And yet we could not even agree to put these on the table along with everything else as we move forward in our efforts to reduce the deficit.

WEAKENS OUR ABILITY TO INVEST

As I have observed, the balanced budget amendment would largely deny to the Federal government a basic practice that most businesses, families, and states and local governments use — borrowing to finance investments with a long-term payoff. Borrowing to finance new investments is standard business practice. A business that failed to modernize because it could not borrow would soon be left behind.

We must continue to invest in our people. Our economy is creating new jobs at a near-record pace — over five million in the last two years alone — yet it doesn't give much help to those ordinary working families who are at the bottom, or in the struggling middle class. As one Iron Ranger in Minnesota recently told me, "All these jobs being created doesn't do me much good if I have to hold three of them to keep my family together." His comment reflects the anger and economic insecurity many Americans feel because their personal economic experience doesn't jibe with what Government statistics tell them — that unemployment is down, inflation is in check, and economic growth and productivity are booming. Despite these statistics, standards of living and real wages of workers remain flat, or in slight decline; many are just one downsizing away from layoff, and feel less secure. We must invest in the skills and futures of our people if we are going to turn this situation around.

The amendment would force a scaling back of Government investment in areas where economists stress more investment is needed: infrastructure, education and training, early intervention programs for children, research and development. There is growing evidence we invest too little in these areas and that such under-investment has contributed to our Nation's weak economic performance in recent years.

It is true that for too long the Federal Government has been undisciplined in its borrowing, and that is what threatens our fiscal future. We have a responsibility to future generations to get our fiscal house in order, and to do it the Federal Government has to reprioritize spending in relation to this central question of investment, by re-examining programs across the board and eliminating or scaling back those that are wasteful and unnecessary. We must redesign cumbersome Federal structures to meet the challenges of the information age, of rapidly changing demographics, of our decaying inner cities. We should do this in a way that's fair, open and accountable, without the budget smoke and mirrors that have too often fogged the real choices facing voters.

THE MILITARY
READINESS CRISIS

Baker Spring

Baker Spring is a senior defense policy analyst at the Heritage
Foundation, *a leading Conservative policy institute in Washington,
D.C.*

■ POINTS TO CONSIDER

1. Summarize the impact in dollars of the Clinton Administration military proposals.

2. According to the author, what effect would spending cuts have on troop morale? Assess the significance of troop morale to the military.

3. Discuss why the author feels the Clinton Administration falls short in the spending proposals.

4. What role do you think the author sees for the military budget in a balanced budget debate?

Baker Spring, "Clinton Military Budget Is Menacingly Inadequate," **Human Events**, 19 May 1995: 18. Reprinted by permission from **Human Events**, 422 First Street, S.E., Washington, D.C. 20003.

It is up to Congress to do something about the assault on national security funding.

One of the biggest tasks facing the post-100 days-Congress will be to restore U.S. defense spending at least to a level that will finance President Clinton's own defense plan. Few Americans understand that the Clinton Administration hasn't just cut defense spending — it has refused to propose spending levels that would finance the force called for in its own national security strategy, the "Bottom-Up Review." This shortfall — about $110 billion — will have a devastating effect on combat readiness, troop morale and the quality and effectiveness of American arms.

On top of this, despite repeated promises not to cut defense any further, the President's latest budget proposal would reduce defense spending by 5.3% in 1996 and an additional 4.1% in 1997. In fact, the President's total proposal would slash the defense budget by 10% in real terms during the next five years. Combine this with previous post-Cold War cutbacks and, by the year 2000, the Clinton plan would leave the Pentagon with approximately 43% less money than it had in 1985.

CLINTON CUTBACKS HOLD NATIONAL SECURITY PERILS

The additional cuts will, among other things:

- Lower troop morale and hamper recruitment: Under the Clinton plan, military pay will not keep up with inflation. The administration has requested a 2.4% pay raise for military personnel in 1996 and similar increases in later years. Yet, the Congressional Budget Office estimates inflation will be 3.4% next year. If it remains at that level for the next five years, the average soldier's pay could drop by almost 10% in real terms. These cuts in pay not only will make it more difficult for the services to recruit and retain high-quality personnel, they will badly damage morale.

- Weaken combat readiness: Readiness — the ability of the services to go into battle right now — depends not only on manpower, but having the equipment, ready and operational, needed for the mission. Like military pay, spending on "operations and maintenance" will not keep up with inflation under President Clinton's 1996 budget. Instead of letting these fund-

LESSONS OF THE PAST

The current debate over national-security needs presents a rather distressing spectacle in historical amnesia...The Cold War was the third occasion in this century when the U.S. mobilized to prevent anti-democratic forces from dominating Eurasia. The century began with the challenge posed by German imperialism, and barely a generation later the U.S. was at war again, this time to defeat fascism. The outcome of WWII then set the stage for the anti-communist crusade of the post-war period.

Cliff Sobel and Loren Thompson, "The Readiness Trap," **Policy Review**, Spring 1995: 81.

ing levels drop, the administration should kill the $11 billion in non-defense, pork-barrel spending currently hidden in the Pentagon budget. This money could then be spent on maintaining readiness.

- Deny troops the advanced weapons they need to prevail in battle: Funding for military research and development will drop dramatically in the Clinton defense budget. The Administration requested $36.2 billion for research and development in the current fiscal year. By the year 2000, America will be spending only $25 billion in 1995 dollars. This 30% drop will shrink the pool of technologies from which the next generation of weapons will be drawn. As a result, U.S. armed forces will begin to lose their technological superiority over potential foes. The low-cost victory of the Persian Gulf War, where casualties were kept low because of U.S. technological superiority, could become a thing of the past.

- Assure an armed force too small and weak to win the nation's wars: A 1995 report by the General Accounting Office, the non-partisan auditing arm of Congress, found that the Administration's planned force levels are not sufficient to handle two major regional wars "nearly simultaneously," as promised by the Clinton Pentagon. If the Administration continues to stretch the defense budget too thin, America may be hard-pressed to win even one major regional war.

WILL CONGRESS MAKE UP FOR CLINTON WEAKNESS?

It is up to Congress to do something about the Clinton assault on national security funding. At the very least, to protect American security, Congress should fund military pay and operations and maintenance at the cost of inflation. It should increase funding for research and development to the levels necessary to maintain the U.S. technological edge. And it should reinvest non-defense, pork-barrel funds in national security programs.

Will America be able to defend its interests around the world in the future without being threatened in return — or will it become vulnerable to the whims and threats of the many dangerous forces existing in the world today? Congress has the power to ensure that the country makes the right choice.

READING

16

THE PHANTOM READINESS CRISIS

Center for Defense Information

The Center for Defense Information, Washington, D.C., *promotes awareness of military issues. The Center believes that strong social, economic, political and military components and a healthy environment contribute equally to a nation's security. CDI opposes excessive expenditure for weapons and policies that increase danger of war. Their newsletter is* The Defense Monitor.

■ POINTS TO CONSIDER

1. Contrast the post-1989 military spending cuts of Russia with those of the United States. How does U.S. military spending compare to that of other nations?

2. Discuss the maintenance of global standing forces by the U.S. Why does the author feel it is not necessary to maintain these forces in the post-Cold War Era?

3. Describe the flaws in U.S. weapons development and production.

4. List possible reasons for the absence of a military spending debate. Evaluate the effect of this absence in the discussion of deficit reduction.

Excerpted from "Real National Needs and the Military Budget," and "Ending the Arms Race with Ourselves," **The Defense Monitor,** June 1995: 4-5.

Instead of basing our military spending on the theory that "defense has been cut enough" we ought to look for credible threats to our security.

Each morning the American people read or hear about Congressional plans to balance the budget by cutting programs such as school lunches and Medicare. What many wonder is why President Clinton and the Congress have declared the military budget to be exempt from any cuts. Even worse, many members of Congress are actively campaigning to increase the 1996 military budget submitted to Congress by President Clinton. In making defense a "sacred cow" both the President and the Congress justify their position by claiming that defense has been "cut enough" already.

WHY NO DEBATE?

This agreement, a rarity between these two branches of government, virtually guarantees that there will be no meaningful debate about where to cut military spending and by how much. But in a democratic nation, a re-examination of national priorities requires a hard look at every aspect of the budget, including defense.

Determining the size of our military budget on the theory that it has been "cut enough" is obviously based on examining only past expenditures. That's the wrong approach. The size of the military budget should be based on our current and foreseeable needs rather than historic data. Russia, for instance, decided that the outside threat to its security had been reduced so much that it was justified in reducing its post-1989 defense spending by 80%. By contrast, U.S. military outlays for 1995 are $271.6 billion. In 1989 they were $303.6 billion. This represents a cut of about 10%.

NO THREAT

Instead of basing our military spending on the theory that "defense has been cut enough" we ought to look for credible threats to our security. They are hard to identify. Currently, no nation or group of nations can militarily threaten the United States. Furthermore, military analysts agree that no nation or group of nations can achieve such a capability in the near future. If any nation began to strive for that capability, our intelligence community would know it and we would have time to build up to meet the threat. In the recent past, when the U.S. military has been involved, for example, in Panama, Haiti, Somalia, and even Iraq, it has been voluntarily, not because our national security was substantially threatened.

Our military force structure should be based on identifying credible threats and devising a strategy to deter or defeat those threats. Examining the military budgets of other nations is not a way to identify threats but it can be used to identify the lack of a threat. For instance, the United States cannot really consider North Korea to be a credible threat when its military spending is about $5 billion compared to our $271.6 billion. It is even questionable whether North Korea is a credible threat to South Korea, whose annual military spending is about $14 billion, and whose population is twice that of North Korea.

LARGE STANDING FORCES?

Military spending should not be removed from the debate over national priorities. Historically the United States has not maintained large standing military forces. Our nation was built by using our natural and human resources for nonmilitary purposes. We have relied on building up our military power when necessary to meet international challenges. Only in the post-World War II and Korean War periods did we become convinced that the threat of international Communism justified large standing military forces. Communism, however, is no longer a threat. As a form of government, unreconstructed Communism cannot feed its people or compete in the current consumer-oriented, hi-tech world. The collapse of the Soviet Union eliminated the international Communist military threat.

It is appropriate at this time, therefore, that we examine critically our present commitment to raise and maintain large standing military forces. Even lacking a credible military threat, our current Congress seems more committed to large military forces than to health care for all of our citizens, Social Security, school lunches, support for public radio, or support for the arts. What does that say about our society?

If the American people do not want their nation to be the world's policeman, the military budget should be sharply reduced and the funds used to deal more effectively with pressing domestic threats to our national security, such as our growing national debt. The President and the Congress should not deny the American people the right to such a debate.

ENDING THE ARMS RACE WITH OURSELVES

During 45 years of the Cold War, the United States engaged in a heated arms race with the Soviet Union. Now it appears that America is engaged in an arms race with itself. Incredibly, this race is actually heating up in a bidding war between the Clinton White House and a Republican Congress committed under the Contract with America to increase military spending.

Not only does our present military budget approach the combined military budgets of all of the other nations in the world, it is planned to rise from $264 billion this year to $287 billion by 2001 under the budget President Clinton submitted to Congress in February 1995. This is in the race of drastically reduced spending by Russia as well as by our closest friends and allies. Total military spending by the six nations frequently pointed to by the Pentagon as potential enemies (Iraq, Iran, Libya, Syria, North Korea, and Cuba) is about $15 billion a year, or only 6% of the U.S. military budget.

A primary reason put forward to justify this massive disparity in spending is that we must continue to modernize our forces in order to retain technological dominance in weaponry. This proposition needs careful examination. Most of the new U.S. weapons now in production or under development were originally proposed as necessary to defeat the Soviet Union in the 21st century...

WEAPONS SUPERIORITY

The lack of any significant military challenges to U.S. forces provides arguments for saving huge sums by delaying, or canceling outright, further investments in unneeded weapons. Our fighters, bombers, and warships today are superior in quality and capabilities to any existing or potential counterparts in the world well into the 21st Century. Furthermore, if expensive new weapons are produced, it will be necessary to retire first class weapons long before the end of their useful service life.

Examples of this problem highlight the egregious waste which will result under present production plans. The Air Force now plans to build 442 F-22 fighters at a cost of $71.5 billion. It they do so, they must start early retirement of F-15 fighters well before the year 2014 when the first of approximately 900 now flying will begin reaching the end of normal service. Today's F-15 is the finest air superiority fighter ever built and no challenger will exist before the year 2014, if then...

Perhaps the most wasteful proposal of all is to build at least 20 more B-2 stealth bombers. Current plans require the Air Force to maintain a fleet of 100 long-range heavy bombers to carry out a two-war strategy. A recent Air Force study shows that if they acquire an additional 20 B-2 aircraft at an estimated life-cycle cost of $30 billion, they would have to retire their entire fleet of 94 B-1B bombers which are less than 10 years old. Another option would be to retire 94 B-52 bombers which were used in heavy attacks against Iraq in 1991. The B-1Bs have an expected service life until 2018 and the upgraded B-52s could be used until 2030.

If Congress is really serious about balancing the budget, a very good place to start would be to examine the wisdom of turning warships into razor blades and putting first class aircraft in storage long before their useful service life has ended. The potential savings available by retaining the weapons already bought and paid for could exceed $50 billion over the next six years. Continuing programs to create unneeded costly new weapons only puts us in a wasteful arms race with ourselves.

RECOGNIZING AUTHOR'S POINT OF VIEW

This activity may be used as an individualized study guide for students in libraries and resource centers or as a discussion catalyst in small group and classroom discussions.

The capacity to recognize an author's point of view is an essential reading skill. Many readers do not make clear distinctions between descriptive articles that relate factual information and articles that express a point of view. Think about the readings in Chapter Two. Are these readings essentially descriptive articles that relate factual information or articles that attempt to persuade through editorial commentary and analysis?

Guidelines

1. Read through the following source descriptions. Choose one of the source descriptions that best describes each reading in Chapter Two.

Source Descriptions

a. Essentially an article that relates factual information
b. Essentially an article that expresses editorial points of view
c. Both of the above
d. None of the above

2. After careful consideration, pick out one source in Chapter Two that you agree with the most.

3. Summarize the author's point of view in one sentence for each of the following readings:

Reading 5 _____

_____

_____

Reading 6 _____

_____

_____

Reading 7 _____

_____

_____

Reading 8 _____

_____

_____

Reading 9 _____

_____

_____

Reading 10 _____

_____

_____

Reading 11 _____

_____

_____

5. Make up one sentence statements that would be an example of each of the following: **sex bias, race bias, ethnocentric bias, political bias** and **religious bias**.

CHAPTER 3

THE ROLE OF GOVERNMENT

READING

17

THE HARM THAT GOVERNMENT DOES

Robert Genetski

Robert Genetski, of Robert Genetski & Associates, Inc., gave this testimony before the Joint Economic Committee in June 1995.

■ **POINTS TO CONSIDER**

1. Describe the three economic waves that the author discusses.

2. Discuss the author's criticism of the FDR Administration.

3. What harm does Genetski find in shifting power to government?

4. Analyze how the Contract with America represents positive change for the author. Does he find any flaws with the Contract?

5. Evaluate the support the author gives for increased privatization.

Excerpted from the testimony of Robert Genetski before the United States Joint Economic Committee, June 12, 1995.

Throughout most of its history, U.S. economic policies placed maximum power and responsibility in the hands of individuals.

Broad economic movements occur in waves. For fifty years these waves focused on shifting responsibility away from individuals and toward government. At the beginning of the 1980s, the waves began to shift in the opposite direction. The Contract with America represents the second wave of a major transfer in power from government back to individuals.

The Contract is not an end in itself. It is an interim move that will be followed by a more significant and powerful third wave. It is this wave that will form the basis for the economy in the 21st century. The third wave will produce a major boost to productivity and living standards. In the process, it will place the U.S. economy in a position of unsurpassed prosperity.

SHIFTING POWER TO GOVERNMENT

Classical economic principles extol the importance of the individual in creating prosperity. Throughout most of its history, U.S. economic policies placed maximum power and responsibility in the hands of individuals. Policies began to shift away from these pro-growth, classical principles in three waves. The first wave came in response to the Great Depression. A frightened public began to rely more on government and less on individual initiative in an attempt to restore prosperity and economic security. Government programs, such as Social Security, began on a fairly modest scale. As they grew, these programs produced a major shift in power from individuals to government.

In the aftermath of World War II there was a major retrenchment in the power of government. Still, the seeds of government control over the lives of individuals were taking root. The Social Security system grew relentlessly, shifting power from individuals to government. Also, the experience from the Depression years left many with a view that if serious problems arose, government could solve them.

By the late 1960s, policies allowing for government control over the lives of individuals entered a second wave. Government control over retirement income was extended to include control over the funding of health care for retirees. Government also assumed

Reprinted by permission: *Tribune Media Services*

responsibility for health care for the poor as well as countless other responsibilities that were previously left to individuals.

The final wave of government control occurred during President Carter's Administration. Government responsibility extended to the creation of jobs, incomes, safety, energy and the environment. The more government tried to accomplish, the more living standards deteriorated. Instead of living standards doubling every thirty years, by the late 1970s, living standards were rapidly declining.

The experiment with higher tax rates and a greater reliance on government was a costly failure. Instead of productivity growing at 2% to 2.5% a year as it had historically, growth slowed to virtually nothing by the end of the 1970s. Each year of poor productivity meant less income for U.S. workers.

Productivity is the key to living standards. When productivity falters, living standards suffer. Although real worker compensation may increase faster or slower than productivity for a limited time, eventually the two must move together. With productivity increasing at 2.25% a year, the real value of a worker's salary would double every thirty years. With the shift in power and responsibility to government, by the late 1970s, productivity stopped growing.

Had greater and greater responsibilities not been taken from individuals, the inefficiencies associated with government would not have occurred. U.S. productivity in 1981 would have been roughly 13% higher than it actually was. This means that total compensation per full-time worker would have been roughly $37,000 in 1981 instead of $32,700. Since there were 88 million full-time equivalent workers in 1981, the experiment with big government cost the economy almost $400 billion in lost output in 1981 alone. (All figures are in 1993 dollars.)

RESTORING POWER TO INDIVIDUALS

The deterioration in living standards in the late 1970s led to a backlash against government. What followed was the first wave of a broad historical movement back toward pro-growth classical principles. In 1981, President Reagan began to reverse almost fifty years of government intrusion. Critics of the first wave complained about many of the changes. They argued that the tax cuts benefited the rich, that government spending and regulation continued to grow rapidly, and that reforms in the Social Security system placed more power than ever in the hands of government.

While all of these criticisms were valid, they missed a sense of what was happening. For the first time in half a century, the American people were beginning to question whether a more powerful government was an asset or a liability. In 1989 the first wave came to an end. During the years 1981-89 living standards for the typical worker had increased by anywhere from 7% to 12% depending upon the measures used. This was the first significant increase in living standards in twenty years and provided the first hint of the direction future policies would take.

Few leaders in either party realized the significance of the first wave. Some complained that whatever improvement occurred was the result of increased government debt. Oddly enough, they chose to associate the improvement in productivity with an increase in government debt. Actually, the productivity improvement in the 80s came in spite of more government debt. The increase in government debt resulted primarily from a failure to control the growth in government spending.

Many observers failed to recognize the role of lower tax and regulatory burdens in improving productivity and living standards in the 1980s. As a result, the first wave was followed by a move backward. From 1989 to 1994, major new tax and regulatory burdens were placed on the economy. Productivity faltered and living standards quickly reversed their upward trend.

The second wave emerged from the setback of the past five years. The Contract with America is the main symbol of this wave. As with the first wave, this one has its shortcomings. The focus on the goal of a balanced budget threatens to do more harm than good.

If the arguments about the negative effects of the deficit on future generations are correct, then cutting taxes makes no sense at all. Fortunately for the sake of overburdened taxpayers, the arguments about the damage from government debt are not valid. My research indicates that tax cuts may well lead to lower government revenues within the first five years. However, tax cuts also lead to higher private incomes. In the wake of the tax cuts in the early 80s, private incomes rose by $3.50 for every dollar of lost revenue to the government.

As with the first wave, focusing on the shortcomings of the present movement misses the significance of what is happening. The second wave is attempting to shift power from government to individuals as quickly as possible. The family tax credit and the focus on cutting government spending are designed to accomplish this objective.

THE THIRD WAVE

The third wave will permanently shift vast amounts of power and responsibility from government to individuals. The broad outlines of the third wave are already emerging in different areas. The move toward term limits is characteristic of the third wave. Term limits provide further incentives for politicians to shift vast amounts of power and influence from government to individuals. In the third wave, politicians will serve brief periods in government and then have to work under the laws they created.

A low, flat rate tax is another characteristic of the third wave. This simple change would save over $100 billion a year in direct costs and more than another $100 billion in indirect costs. Every bit as important as these savings is the transfer of power that accompanies such a change. Rather than lobbying Congress for tax favors, a simple, flat tax would enable those in the private sector to devote all their time and energy toward producing their output as efficiently as possible.

In the third wave the responsibility for health care will be placed primarily with individuals, not with government or insurance companies or HMOs. Instead of serving third parties, doctors and hospitals will be able to serve their new customers — their patients.

Another major policy change in the third wave will be the privatization of Social Security. This move will get its impetus from Chile's experience. Chile privatized its social security system in 1981 and the results have been astonishing. In less than ten years from now the typical Chilean worker (whose annual income is roughly $5,400) will have more assets in a retirement account alone than the total assets of the typical American family. Few policy makers will want to explain to their constituents why they refuse to support a similar plan for U.S. citizens.

One of the most exciting aspects of the third wave is the implication for productivity and living standards. The structural changes in the third wave will not just improve productivity performance to match the 2% to 2.5% trends of history. Rather, productivity performance will surpass its historical trends as the new move toward efficiency makes up for the inefficiencies of the past 30 years. Instead of simply doubling in the next 30 years, living standards can be expected to increase by one and a half times their current level.

When the final wave has ended, the United States of America will truly fulfill the dreams of the Founding Fathers. More so than at any time in its history, the country will be a land of plenty, a land of unsurpassed opportunity.

READING

18

THE GOOD THAT GOVERNMENT DOES

Dane Smith

Dane Smith has been a state politics and government reporter for the
Star Tribune *since 1986. He has covered local, state and federal government and politics for 15 years, including three years as the*
Washington *correspondent for the* St. Paul Pioneer Press. *As one of a
three-part newspaper series, he wrote the following out of a desire to
atone for what he describes as a decade and a half of government
bashing, including a series in 1988 that criticized the rapid growth of
state and local government spending over a two-decade period.*

■ POINTS TO CONSIDER

1. What reasons does the author cite for the dissatisfaction with government?

2. Summarize some of the strides the government has made in areas
   of space, science and technology.

3. Assess the author's point about government funding of infrastructure.

4. Discuss the positive gains the government has made through environmental regulation.

Dane Smith, "The Good that Government Does," **Star Tribune,** 17 Jan. 1994: 9A.
Reprinted with permission of the **Star Tribune**, Minneapolis-St. Paul.

A historical evaluation of the performance of federal, state and local governments reveals an impressive record of missions accomplished, problems solved and conditions improved during the past half-century.

From the bureaucratic sinkholes in Washington, to the free-spending agencies at the Capitol in St. Paul, to the tab-grabbing city halls and school districts across the Twin Cities, the evidence is overwhelming. Governments can't do anything right, and they're confiscating more and more of our money toward that end. The public sector is coercive, inefficient and bloated, a black hole that sucks up our hard-earned money for no good purpose. Taxes and government spending are out of control and must be slashed.

Many Americans feel this way at least some of the time, but increasingly one hears unqualified government bashing. Not only that government "isn't the answer," but that it is mostly ineffective, totally unproductive, or actually worsens problems it attempts to solve.

And that's not fair.

There's a completely different perspective, seldom presented in a comprehensive way even by defenders of the public sector, that affords a view of a government glass that's far more than half full. While governments are taking a bigger bite out of our paychecks than they were 20 years ago (although not as much more as some might think and not as much as in most other industrialized democracies), a historical evaluation of the performance of federal, state and local governments reveals an impressive record of missions accomplished, problems solved and conditions improved during the past half-century.

Consider:

- The federal government in the past 50 years has delivered two global victories over totalitarianism, World War II and the 40-year Cold War.

- Through Social Security and Medicaid and Medicare, federal and state governments have dramatically reduced poverty for the elderly, even as that portion of the population has grown in numbers and longevity.

120

- Governments working together have both led and responded to one of the greatest social justice revolutions in human history, the liberation and elevation of minorities and women and every manner of handicapped — two-thirds of the U.S. population.

- Governments have built and maintained an impressive public works infrastructure of highways, sewers, airports and water projects, without which businesses could not exist.

- The public sector since the early 1970s has pushed through a clean-up of a fouled environment that threatened the health and welfare of humans and all other life.

- Government now delivers perhaps half again as much education, in terms of average time spent in class per citizen, than it did 50 years ago, and has helped build what is widely considered the finest higher education system in the world.

Exhibit by exhibit, here's the case for the defense of a grossly maligned American public sector, with Minnesota as one of its biggest spending and most productive provinces.

HOT AND COLD RUNNING WARS

Unimaginable sums of tax money — about $16 trillion — have been poured into defense since 1941, according to the Center for Defense Information. Liberals, normally defenders of government spending, have nonetheless been the biggest critics of this spending, claiming that world communism would have failed without the bloodshed of Korea and Vietnam and the arms race. And nobody can be happy about the unending scandals over $500 toilet seats, zillion-dollar airplanes that won't fly and wholesale rip-offs by some defense contractors.

Necessary or not, the fact is that a clear majority of Americans throughout this period supported a policy of containment, deterrence and military intervention when needed. Presidential candidates who even hinted that they were less than gung-ho — not willing, in the words of President John F. Kennedy, to "pay any price" — were soundly defeated.

The bottom line is that victory was attained in two global struggles. Pentagon bureaucrats and government employees led the rout of fascism and communism, which represented a real threat to democracy and, at times it seemed, the survival of the species.

Other good things happened along the way. War and defense spending created one of the great public employment projects of all times, one that created prosperity for millions of families and entire regions, most notably Southern California. Military service continues to serve as a relief valve for youths with few other options.

Even as the defense budget began to shrink in 1990, uniformed and civilian employees numbered 3.9 million strong, earning about $100 billion. The trillions of dollars that went to military contractors sustained other millions of families in the private sector, partially or entirely for five decades. As recently as 1992, defense businesses took in $117 billion a year. Minnesota got $1.5 billion of that business, along with $358 million for a mostly civilian payroll of about 3,000.

These global wars created an army of almost 27 million veterans by 1992, two million of them partially or totally disabled. By 1992, benefits were running $30 billion a year, mostly for pensions and medical coverage. Not that this provides a lucrative sinecure, however — military retirees' average annual benefits amounted to less than $5,000 in 1992. But the GI Bill's benefits did help house and educate two generations of veterans, a benefit that by consensus helped create a thriving middle class in America.

SPACE BUCKS

The Hubble telescope didn't work at first and the Challenger blew up, but the scope got fixed and only Americans have walked on the moon. Americans are leading the way into the cosmos and the public has been mostly supportive, despite the huge cost. The price was $28 billion in 1991, about half of it defense-related.

A byproduct of incalculable value from both defense and space programs has been the advances in scientific knowledge and technology development. Defense-space programs in the early 1960s accounted for more than half of all money spent on basic research, applied research and development. Even now, with U.S. businesses spending more, the public investment into basic research, much of it sponsored by universities and related to health, exceeds $70 billion, a bit less than half of all R&D money spent in the nation.

KEEPING PACE WITH THE ELDERLY

The public sector has been so successful at alleviating poverty among the elderly — through massive spending on health, housing and direct cash pension benefits — that now this phenomenon is interpreted as a problem. Advocates for other government programs argue that older Americans are too well off, and are consuming benefits that should be going to increasingly impoverished children.

For the record, the percentage of Americans over the age of 65 living in poverty has been sliced in half over just the past two decades, to 12.4 percent in 1991 from 24.6 percent in 1970. Progress on this front was well underway by the early 1970s, with the retirement of the first generation to have worked most of the time under the Social Security system, launched in the 1930s. But government's big step into health care sealed the deal.

State and federal governments were spending more than $300 billion in the early 1990s on Medicare and Medicaid programs, and most of it goes to the elderly. About 50 million Americans and more than one million Minnesotans received these benefits in 1990. This spending, along with heavy public support of medical research, surely had an impact on life expectancy, which continues to inch upward.

ENVIRONMENTAL STRIDES

Businesses and labor unions fought the so-called green revolu-

123

tion at times and still do. But there's a consensus now that the great cleanup of the past two decades was absolutely necessary, a classic example of government's proper role in stepping in to correct a free-market mess.

Between 1970 and 1991, total air emissions of carbon monoxide in the United States have been reduced by half, sulfur oxides by about a fourth, particulates by more than a third, and highly toxic lead by 97 percent. Rivers that once caught fire or were discolored grotesquely with effluents now swarm with fish and healthy plant life. The number of streams with unacceptable fecal coliform bacteria has been reduced by a third to a half since the late 1970s. Oil polluting incidents in and around U.S. waters have been reduced from 10,000-12,000 per year in the early 1970s to 6,000-9,000 in recent years.

Recycling, initiated and financed by local governments, has boosted the percentage of recovered waste from 7.1 percent in 1970 to 17.1 percent in 1990. Minnesota governments have been a national leader in this effort. Higher taxes on energy and other government-sponsored efforts have helped make the United States far more energy efficient. The economy consumes about a third less energy than it did in 1970 to produce the same amount of goods and services.

The total public cost of environmental programs is big potatoes, reaching about $21 billion in 1990. Much greater costs have been borne by polluters and their customers, an estimated $64 billion annually. Still, as with defense, jobs have been created. Environmental industries employed almost 1.1. million people and earned revenues of $134 billion in 1992.

A NATION'S BUILDING BLOCKS

America's public works systems were once the envy of the world. Even though competing nations such as Japan and France have caught up with their bullet trains and other improvements, public investment in the bricks and asphalt and pipes that connect our communities has been a major factor in the U.S. stature as an economic superpower.

About $157 billion was spent in 1991 by all governments, excluding the Defense Department, on physical structures and public works. These include new construction and rehab of highways and streets, schools and college buildings, highways, hospitals, parks, housing, airports, waterways, irrigation, libraries, sewerage and solid waste disposal facilities, and mass transit systems.

At a cost of about $80 billion in 1992, governments maintained 3.9 million miles of highways and streets — 129,000 miles in Minnesota, one of the largest rural farm-to-market networks in the country and a significant factor in the state's high-tax status. Everybody gripes about potholes, and pavement conditions as measured by the Federal Highway Administration have deteriorated on both rural and urban interstates, a 45,000-mile system that stands as a crowning achievement of U.S. public works know-how.

But that's only part of the story. Increased gasoline taxes and big spending in response to an early '80s fear of an "infrastructure crisis" have improved the condition of urban residential streets and both major and minor routes in rural areas. In Minnesota, the number of bridges rated as deficient has been whittled from 5,400 in 1977 to 3,875 in 1993, even though the standards for bridge safety and efficiency have been toughened, according to the Minnesota Department of Transportation.

Government's vital role in public infrastructure was established almost at the birth of the nation, with the federal government taking the lead in building roads, canals and subsidizing railroad development. This role was expanded enormously during the Great Depression, when the father of big government, Franklin D. Roosevelt, used public works not only to build things but also as an employment program. Public support of such projects, despite criticism from post-1960s liberals about environmental damage and unfair subsidies to businesses, traditionally has been high.

IMPERFECTIONS

These feathers in the federal cap must be balanced against some disappointing failures, which have been amply documented and have helped to foster a bold contempt of government. These include the bloodshed of the Vietnam War, the frustrating spread of urban poverty and crime despite anti-poverty programs, the ludicrous inability of Congress to control the federal budget.

At a personal and local level, too many of us have had at least some first-hand visions of bad government: big tax grabs by local governments, the incompetent school teacher who can't be fired, the stupid zoning rules, the neighbor who abuses the welfare system or workers' compensation, the local politicians caught feathering their nests.

But these frustrations must be balanced against the larger picture and a record of government achievement that can't be denied. "I don't see government as good or bad. I see it as indispensable," says John Kenneth Galbraith, the noted economist and longtime advocate of the public sector who appears to be making something of a comeback in national policy circles at the age of 85. Galbraith added in a recent Associated Press interview: "It's not a question of whether government is efficient or inefficient. It's a question of making it better, because there's no alternative."

A CONTRACT ON OUR ENVIRONMENT

John Sterling

John Sterling is the associate editor of Earth Island Journal, *the quarterly publication of the Earth Island Institute, San Francisco, California. Earth Island Institute is a prominent national and international environmental organization.*

■ POINTS TO CONSIDER

1. Summarize the effect of the Job Creation and Wage Enhancement Act.

2. According to the poll, what kind of support do environmental laws have among the American people?

3. Evaluate the article's stance on the "cost-benefit" test.

4. Why does the author state that the "Contract [with America] puts the environment on the defensive"?

John Sterling, "Contract on the Environment," **Earth Island Journal**, Summer, 1995: 32. Reprinted with permission from Earth Island Institute.

Most Americans believe that protecting endangered species is more important than safeguarding corporate profits.

When the first 100 days of the 104th Congress expired, the Republican's "Contract with America" was still plodding through the legislative process. Despite House Speaker Newt Gingrich's legislative blitz, citizens opposed to the GOP agenda voiced their opposition to the Contract, which stands as a major threat to the environment.

"The entire environmental movement is at stake right now," warned Gary Bass, director of the Office of Management and Budget (OMB) Watch, which monitors the Office of Management and Budget. Bass was referring to the threat posed by the Job Creation and Wage Enhancement Act (JCWEA), item eight of the ten-point Contract, which would cripple government regulatory agencies, leaving corporations free to run roughshod over existing environmental laws.

"This act would have an enormous environmental impact, because the environmental movement relies so heavily on government safeguards and protections," said Bass. "It is a clever bill, because it does not openly attack laws, but instead strangles the process by which regulations are created and enforced."

ENVIRONMENTAL IMPACT

The Contract operates under the assumption that all government regulation is bad. With its anti-regulatory agenda, the JCWEA would emasculate the Endangered Species Act, the Clean Water Act, the Clean Air Act and the Superfund Toxic Cleanup Law. These laws, passed in the public interest, sometimes interfere with corporate profitability.

Most Americans believe that protecting endangered species is more important than safeguarding corporate profits. Because business has no inherent interest in protecting the environment (unless it is profitable to do so), that responsibility lies with government. If passed, the JCWEA would drastically impair government's ability to regulate environmentally damaging practices.

The act would begin by cutting the budgets of government agencies that implement and enforce regulations by 6.5 percent per year for seven years and then capping the cost of all subse-

ROOSEVELT'S VISION

I admire Teddy Roosevelt for many reasons, but one of the most important is that he taught us the necessity of preserving our natural resources and protecting our natural world. He established the National Wildlife Refuges. The Forest Service grew in size and vision under his leadership. His actions led to the creation of the National Park Service, which takes care of this very park.

Excerpted from the comments of President William Clinton concerning the Clean Water Act; Rock Creek Park, Washington, D.C., May 30, 1995.

quent regulations at a total of 3-5 percent of the U.S. Gross Domestic Product (GDP). The current cost of federal regulations is estimated at roughly 8.5 percent of the GDP, or $500 billion annually.

Once a bill becomes law, it is assigned to a specific House or Senate committee (i.e. the Clean Water Act falls under the jurisdiction of the Environment Committee). Federal agencies in turn enforce the laws by imposing regulations. Under the JCWEA, each Congressional committee would be assigned a two-year budget that agencies may spend to enforce the laws under that committee's jurisdiction. Once a committee expended its regulatory budget, it could bring no new legislation to the floor unless three-fifths of the House or the Senate voted to waive this restriction. Under this scenario, "there is virtually no chance that any future environmental protections will be passed," said OMB Watch's Bass.

The House or Senate Budget Committees could decide, by a simple majority, to slash the budgets of committees that oversee critical environmental legislation. If a new environmental bill did make it to the House or Senate floor, it would then be open to judicial review, whereby the industries to be regulated could threaten costly legal challenges to block proposed regulations before they even become law.

COST-BENEFIT

The JCWEA would also resurrect Ronald Reagan's "cost-benefit" test, under which an agency that proposes, say, a regulation to ensure clean water, would first have to prove that the financial benefits of clean water would be worth more than the cost for business to comply. In effect, the degree to which we protect the environment would be determined on business' terms.

The Wise Use-backed "takings" provision of the JCWEA would require the government to compensate property owners if a regulation reduces the value of their property by as little as ten percent. Owners now must pursue compensation through the courts. Under the JCWEA, any property owner could simply request compensation from the agency responsible for the regulation and that agency would be required to offer payment within six months.

The takings provision would give polluting industries the power to intimidate government regulators with threats to sue for lost profits and the costs of emissions-control equipment. Government agencies would be reluctant to impose new regulations for fear that they would spend much of their shrinking budgets compensating polluting industries.

ENVIRONMENT ON DEFENSIVE

The Contract puts the environment on the defensive. Rather than forcing companies to prove that business practices do not harm the environment, it requires government and financially strapped nonprofits, to prove that environmental protections do not harm business. If the JCWEA passes, business will accelerate the rate at which it profits at the expense of the environment...

Bass insists that citizens should continue to pressure their representatives in both the House and the Senate. "Even though the Senate is the short-term concern, the battles need to be fought in both chambers. Remember that any legislation that the President vetoes must go back to both the House and the Senate."

The Contract does not have the overwhelming support of the American people. According to a poll commissioned by the National Wildlife Federation, 41 percent of those who voted in the November election think environmental laws are too weak and another 21 percent believed these laws should stay as they are. Only 18 percent feel that existing environmental regulations are too stringent. But the JCWEA could pass and wreak environmental havoc if the public does not challenge it now.

READING

20

RESTORING A BALANCE TO ENVIRONMENTAL POLICY

Doug Bandow

Doug Bandow is a nationally syndicated columnist. He is a senior fellow at the Cato Institute, Washington, D.C. and the author of The Politics of Envy: Statism as Theology.

■ POINTS TO CONSIDER

1. Discuss what the author means by "balance" in environmental policy.

2. Summarize the justifications for eased regulations.

3. Contrast the regulation compliance costs of 1972 with today, as cited in the reading.

4. Describe how, as the author states, environmental laws may in some cases actually hurt rather than help the environment.

Doug Bandow, "Restore a Balance to Environmental Policy," © *1995 Copley News Service.* Reprinted by permission from *Copley News Service.*

America's rigid environmental rules are unnecessarily expensive.

"We are witnessing the most extreme and concerted assault on the environment in history," warned Vice President Al Gore in a speech at George Washington University. House Republicans, he complained, are engaged in "a deliberate attack" on decades worth of environmental legislation.

Why is the Vice President so upset? The GOP wants to require that agencies balance the costs and benefits of regulations. That science be consulted to assess the relative risk of alternative actions. That citizens be compensated when government effectively seizes their property. And that new rules be suspended while Congress reviews the laws that have led to so much abusive bureaucratic behavior. Is this really so unreasonable?

While the Vice President is steadfastly defending the bureaucratic state, President Bill Clinton is, as usual, searching for the middle ground. Although he attacks the House legislation as "unacceptable," the President has ordered his appointees to develop a list of obsolete rules for repeal and create a culture of "negotiation" with those they regulate.

That would be better than nothing, but not much. Over the past 25 years, Uncle Sam has spun webs of legal restrictions, turning many businessmen and property owners into *de facto* vassals of the state. The government has spent billions of dollars — and made the American people spend literally hundreds of billions of dollars more — making dirt safe to eat, prosecuting people for cleaning up dry "wetlands," eliminating miniscule amounts of auto emissions, and undertaking a host of similar follies.

RISING COSTS

Total compliance costs have skyrocketed from $31 billion (in 1990 dollars) in 1972 to about $150 billion today. Add the cost of state and local rules as well as of the regulators themselves, and total outlays run some $200 billion annually. Environmental spending is not only increasing, it also is accounting for an ever-greater share of overall regulatory costs. According to Thomas Hopkins of the Rochester Institute of Technology, in 1977 environmental dictates represented just 7.8 percent of total compliance costs. That share jumped to 18.4 percent in 1988 and 21.2 percent in 1991, and is expected to hit 26.9 percent by 2000.

Moreover, these numbers badly understate the overall effect of federal environmental rules. The real question is: what is the value of the production foregone as a result of regulation? What if American business had been able to invest an extra $30 billion or $40 billion year in and year out? One estimate, from economist Bill Laffer, is that the standard figures understate true regulatory costs by a factor of two or three. A 1989 study by professors Dale Jorgenson and Peter Wilcoxen concluded that auto production alone was 15 percent lower than it otherwise would have been.

UNNECESSARY EXPENSE

The mere fact that regulation is expensive doesn't necessarily mean it is bad, of course. Unfortunately, however, America's rigid environmental rules are unnecessarily expensive. European nations and Japan also value clean environments; they, however, spend far less on regulation. For instance, American outlays are twice those of the entire 12-member European Community.

Indeed, Uncle Sam has managed to produce a set of rules unique in their perversity. The EPA has problems deciding what substances to measure and how to measure them. The agency plays fast and loose with official pollution levels in order to justify more Draconian regulation.

Washington refused to allow different regions to set different standards. Legislators routinely use environmental requirements to enrich special interests, such as Archer Daniels Midland and other alcohol fuel manufacturers. Laws like the Endangered Species Act actually encourage property owners to destroy environmental habitat, lest the government use it as an excuse to seize control of their land.

Finally, until now, at least, Congress has refused to consider whether its actions make economic sense: the 1990 Clean Air Act was passed despite estimates that it would cost between 13 and 50 times its benefits! It is this regulatory miasma, then, and not the environment, that the House has attacked. And the newly passed legislation is merely a start — Congress needs to revisit every environmental statute, requiring use of sound science, constraining bureaucratic authority, mandating reliance on market solutions and emphasizing the importance of balance.

In fact, "balance" should be the GOP's theme as the Senate now takes up the issue of regulatory reform. In recent years Uncle Sam has grown slightly crazed, seemingly committed to wrecking the economy in order to satisfy a few environmental extremists who really would prefer to live in Medieval times than today. Congress must restore balance to environmental policy, demanding that regulators recognize the importance of economic growth and individual liberty.

READING

21

AFFIRMATIVE ACTION: THE POINT

Adam Meyerson

Adam Meyerson is the editor of Policy Review, *the quarterly publication of the Heritage Foundation. The Heritage Foundation is a public policy institute that promotes conservative economic and political ideas.*

■ POINTS TO CONSIDER

1. Summarize the moral or ethical arguments against affirmative action.

2. In what ways does affirmative action hurt business and entrepreneurship?

3. Discuss the author's statement that something "must be done instead of racial preferences, or a generation of black men will be destroyed."

4. According to Meyerson, what effect do lower performance standards have on children?

Adam Meyerson, "Nixon's Ghost," **Policy Review**, Summer 1995: 4-5. Reprinted by permission from **Policy Review**.

Racial preferences are discriminatory. It is just as wrong for the government to discriminate in favor of blacks and other minorities as it is to discriminate against them.

A generation has passed since the Nixon administration established racial quotas in hiring, promotion, college admissions and government contracting. Affirmative action policies, both public and private, have opened many economic and educational opportunities for African Americans, and have played an important role in one of the most encouraging developments of recent decades: the emergence of a large and growing black middle class. But supporters of government-mandated racial preferences have always been uncomfortable about policies that judge Americans by the color of their skin, not the content of their character — the opposite of Martin Luther King Jr.'s dream. Even if racial preferences have been justified on a temporary basis, they surely cannot be justified for more than a generation.

Citizens and politicians are beginning to roll quotas back. Senators Bob Dole and Phil Gramm both have promised that, if elected president, they would repeal President Nixon's executive order requiring all government contractors to submit detailed "goals and timetables" for the hiring and promotion of minorities and women. Governor Pete Wilson has abolished some racial hiring quotas established by California law. Even President Clinton is reviewing the issue.

Perhaps the most dramatic movement is the California Civil Rights Initiative, which enjoys overwhelming support in public-opinion polls. The brainchild of two scholars, Glynn Custred and Thomas Wood, the initiative is based on the color-blind language of the Civil Rights Act of 1964: "Neither the State of California nor any of its political subdivisions or agents shall use race, sex, color, ethnicity or national origin as a criterion for either discriminating against, or granting preferential treatment to, any individual or group in the operation of the State's system of public employment, public education or public contracting."

GAINING GROUND

There are six reasons why the repeal of government-mandated racial quotas is gaining the support of the American people:

Reprinted by permission of *Copley News Service.*

- Racial preferences are discriminatory. It is just as wrong for the government to discriminate in favor of blacks and other minorities as it is to discriminate against them. Preferring one race to another is a violation of the Declaration of Independence, which holds that all men are created equal; of the 14th Amendment, which guarantees all citizens the equal protection of the laws; and of the Civil Rights Act of 1964, which explicitly forbids government-mandated reverse discrimination. This discrimination has real victims, such as the Asians denied admission to the University of California in spite of spectacular records, and would-be policemen and firemen who lose jobs to applicants who are substantially less qualified.

- Racial preferences violate the principles of American citizenship. Americans come from all races, all religions, all nationalities. What unites us as a nation is not a common origin, but a common commitment to our political institutions: the rights to life, liberty, and the pursuit of happiness; the Constitution; a self-governing republic. Martin Luther King Jr. brought Americans together — by speaking of what Americans have in common, by showing how the civil-rights movement fit into the American political tradition. Racial preferences do the opposite; they balkanize our country by emphasizing our differences.

137

- Racial preferences foster dependency on government. Ronald Reagan used to say that "the success of welfare should be judged by how many of its recipients become independent of welfare." So, too, the success of affirmative action should be judged by how many businesses become independent of set-asides, by how many individuals become independent of quotas in promotion and hiring. Unfortunately, all too many businesses have become part of a permanent affirmative action industry.

- Racial preferences restrict freedom. Much of the creativity of a market economy comes from the freedom that individuals and businesses have to discover and use information. Bureaucratic, highly regulated affirmative action policies endanger this creativity by denying businesses the freedom to hire and fire whomever they wish.

MINORITIES IN THE MAINSTREAM

- Racial preferences fail to address the central challenge facing black America today: integrating poor black males into the American mainstream. The number of black men in college has fallen behind even as affirmative action preferences in college admissions have intensified: There are now only 540,000 African-American men in college, compared with 830,000 black women. The explosion of violent crime by young black men wasn't supposed to happen with affirmative action. Something drastically different must be done instead of racial preferences, or a generation of black men will be destroyed.

- Most perniciously, racial preferences lower standards and expectations. When African Americans and Hispanics are held to a lower standard than members of other groups, the implicit message is patronizing, even racist. The signal sent by different treatment is that African Americans and Hispanics cannot compete on their own, unless they are given a special handicap. To make matters worse, the very idea of standards is devalued in the culture of affirmative action, where a test is considered discriminatory if blacks and Hispanics don't score well.

PERFORMANCE STANDARDS

It is no accident that the two institutions in which blacks have advanced the most rapidly in America, the military and athletics, are meritocracies with clear performance standards. Colin Powell did not become the chairman of the Joint Chiefs of Staff and one of the outstanding generals in American history by receiving special treatment in his performance reviews. The military, it is frequently said, is the only institution in America in which blacks regularly give orders to whites. This is because blacks in the armed forces have been given standards to aspire to, and the opportunity to achieve them.

By contrast, public schools in America set tragically low academic expectations for poor children, especially for blacks and Hispanics. The culture of affirmative action reinforces these low expectations, with a defeatist message that minorities can't make the grade, and that standards don't even really matter. The sad fact is that on average, blacks and Hispanics do score poorly on standardized academic tests. But that isn't an indictment of the tests; it's an indictment of the school system and surrounding culture that discourage kids from achieving...

In New York City, the number of black ninth-graders passing the New York State Regents' science exam doubled from 6,000 in 1994 to nearly 13,000 in 1995, while the number of Hispanics passing the test tripled from 3,000 to over 10,000. The difference? In 1995, at the insistence of New York City School Chancellor Ramon Cortines, black and Hispanic students were expected to take Regents-level science courses and succeed in them. Prior to that, they were expected to fail.

Expectations make all the difference for modest levels of achievement as well. During the early 1980s, Florida established a functional literacy test as a criterion of high-school graduation. Florida schools now give diplomas only to students who pass a test measuring whether they can fill out basic job application forms, do the basic kinds of comparison shopping, balance check books, and otherwise participate in a modern society. At first, 80 to 90 percent of black 12th-graders failed. The test was challenged in court by the Legal Services Corp. on the grounds that it was discriminatory. But Florida gives students five chances to sit for the exam, and 90 percent of black 12th-graders now get passing scores. Those graduates are much better off for being forced to achieve a minimum level of competency.

THE BEST AFFIRMATIVE ACTION

The best affirmative action offers opportunities to outsiders without lowering standards and expectations. This means holding the members of all races to the same high standard and, if necessary, giving people the extra training they need to make the grade. It means not reserving particular jobs for blacks. It means making a genuine effort to find African Americans — and other Americans of all races — who might be overlooked but who have the capacity to excel.

AFFIRMATIVE ACTION: THE COUNTERPOINT

Justices John Paul Stevens vs. Ruth Bader Ginsburg

Supreme Court Justice John Paul Stevens was nominated for Associate Justice by President Ford. He has been seated on the court since December 1975. Justice Ruth Bader Ginsburg was nominated by President Clinton for Associate Justice and has been seated since August 1993. Ginsburg joined Stevens in dissent for the case of Adarand Constructors vs. Federico Peña.

■ POINTS TO CONSIDER

1. Explain why Justice Stevens rejects affirmative action opponents' concept of "consistency." What distinguishes affirmative action from policies that impose a negative burden on a racial or ethnic minority?

2. What role does history play in the debate of affirmative action policies?

3. What is the purpose of affirmative action, if not to end racial discrimination, according to Justice Ginsburg?

4. Summarize the intent of "strict scrutiny" as explained by Justice Ginsburg.

Excerpted from the dissenting opinions of Justices John Paul Stevens and Ruth Bader Ginsburg in Adarand Constructors, Inc., Petitioner vs. Federico Peña, Secretary of Transportation, et al., argued January 17, 1995; decided June 12, 1995.

JUSTICE STEVENS, WITH WHOM JUSTICE GINSBURG JOINS, DISSENTING

The Court's concept of "consistency" assumes that there is no significant difference between a decision by the majority to impose a special burden on the members of a minority race and a decision by the majority to provide a benefit to certain members of that minority...In my opinion that assumption is untenable. There is no moral or constitutional equivalence between a policy that is designed to perpetuate a caste system and one that seeks to eradicate racial subordination. Invidious discrimination is an engine of oppression, subjugating a disfavored group to enhance or maintain the power of the majority. Remedial race-based preferences reflect the opposite impulse: a desire to foster equality in society. No sensible conception of the Government's constitutional obligation to "govern impartially" should ignore this distinction.

To illustrate the point, consider our cases addressing the Federal Government's discrimination against Japanese Americans during World War II, Hirabayashi vs. United States, 320 U.S. 81 (1943), and Korematsu vs. United States, 323 U.S. 214 (1944). The discrimination at issue in those cases was invidious because the Government imposed special burdens — a curfew and exclusion from certain areas on the West Coast — on the members of a minority class defined by racial and ethnic characteristics. Members of the same racially defined class exhibited exceptional heroism in the service of our country during that War. Now suppose Congress decided to reward that service with a federal program that gave all Japanese-American veterans an extraordinary preference in Government employment. If Congress had done so, the same racial characteristics that motivated the discriminatory burdens in Hirabayashi and Korematsu would have defined the preferred class of veterans. Nevertheless, "consistency" surely would not require us to describe the incidental burden on everyone else in the country as "odious" or "invidious" as those terms were used in those cases. We should reject a concept of "consistency" that would view the special preferences that the National Government has provided to Native Americans since 1834 as comparable to the official discrimination against African Americans that was prevalent for much of our history.

The consistency that the Court espouses would disregard the difference between a "No Trespassing" sign and a welcome mat. It would treat a Dixiecrat Senator's decision to vote against Thurgood Marshall's confirmation in order to keep African Americans off the Supreme Court as on a par with President

Cartoon by Gary Markstein. Reprinted by permission.

Johnson's evaluation of his nominee's race as a positive factor. It would equate a law that made black citizens ineligible for military service with a program aimed at recruiting black soldiers. An attempt by the majority to exclude members of a minority race from a regulated market is fundamentally different from a subsidy that enables a relatively small group of newcomers to enter that market. An interest in "consistency" does not justify treating differences as though they were similarities...

The term "affirmative action" is common and well understood. Its presence in everyday parlance shows that people understand the difference between good intentions and bad. As with any legal concept, some cases may be difficult to classify, but our equal protection jurisprudence has identified a critical difference between state action that imposes burdens on a disfavored few and state action that benefits the few "in spite of" its adverse effects on the many...

As a matter of constitutional and democratic principle, a decision by representatives of the majority to discriminate against the members of a minority race is fundamentally different from those same representatives' decision to impose incidental costs on the majority of their constituents in order to provide a benefit to a disadvantaged minority. Indeed, as I have previously argued, the former is virtually always repugnant to the principles of a free and democratic society, whereas the latter is, in some circumstances, entirely consistent with the ideal of equality.

143

JUSTICE GINSBURG, WITH WHOM JUSTICE BREYER JOINS, DISSENTING

The statutes and regulations at issue, as the Court indicates, were adopted by the political branches in response to an "unfortunate reality": [t]he unhappy persistence of both the practice and the lingering effects of racial discrimination against minority groups in this country." The United States suffers from those lingering effects because, for most of our Nation's history, the idea that "we are just one race," was not embraced. For generations, our lawmakers and judges were unprepared to say that there is in this land no superior race, no race inferior to any other. In Plessy vs. Ferguson, not only did this Court endorse the oppressive practice of race segregation, but even Justice Harlan, the advocate of a "color-blind" Constitution, stated:

"The white race deems itself to be the dominant race in this country. And so it is, in prestige, in achievements, in education, in wealth and in power. So, I doubt not, it will continue to be for all time, if it remains true to its great heritage and holds fast to the principles of constitutional liberty." Id., at 559 (Harlan, J., dissenting).

Not until Loving vs. Virginia, which held unconstitutional Virginia's ban on interracial marriages, could one say with security that the Constitution and this Court would abide no measure "designed to maintain White Supremacy."

The divisions in this difficult case should not obscure the Court's recognition of the persistence of racial inequality and a majority's acknowledgement of Congress' authority to act affirmatively, not only to end discrimination, but also to counteract discrimination's lingering effects. Those effects, reflective of a system of racial caste only recently ended, are evident in our workplaces, markets, and neighborhoods. Job applicants with identical resumes, qualifications, and interview styles still experience different receptions, depending on their race. White and African-American consumers still encounter different deals. People of color looking for housing still face discriminatory treatment by landlords, real estate agents, and mortgage lenders. Minority entrepreneurs sometimes fail to gain contracts though they are the low bidders, and they are sometimes refused work even after winning contracts. Bias both conscious and unconscious, reflecting traditional and unexamined habits of thought, keeps up barriers that must come down if equal opportunity and nondiscrimination are ever genuinely to become this country's law and practice.

LOSING IDEALISM

The reason for the success of the assault on affirmative action is that the idea of affirmative action has largely lost its idealistic meaning, emanating from a vision of true racial equality, of inclusion of all people in a loving and non-exploitative human community that emerged from the spirit of the civil-rights movement. That idealistic meaning was part of a larger challenge to the alienation that pervades American society, to the selfishness and individualism that is fostered by the competitive marketplace and that makes the creation of loving human relationships and cooperative human community so difficult.

Peter Gabel, "Affirmative Action and Racial Harmony," **Tikkun**, May-June, 1995: 33.

Given this history and its practical consequences, Congress surely can conclude that a carefully designed affirmative action program may help to realize, finally, the "equal protection of the laws" the Fourteenth Amendment has promised since 1868...

Today's decision usefully reiterates that the purpose of strict scrutiny "is precisely to distinguish legitimate from illegitimate uses of race in governmental decision making, to 'differentiate between' permissible and impermissible governmental use of race, to distinguish between a 'No Trespassing' sign and a welcome mat."

Close review also is in order for this further reason. As Justice Souter points out, and as this very case shows, some members of the historically favored race can be hurt by catch-up mechanisms designed to cope with the lingering effects of entrenched racial subjugation. Court review can ensure that preferences are not so large as to trammel unduly upon the opportunities of others or interfere too harshly with legitimate expectations of persons in once-preferred groups.

While I would not disturb the programs challenged in this case, and would leave their improvement to the political branches, I see today's decision as one that allows our precedent to evolve, still to be informed by and responsive to changing conditions.

GOVERNMENT HEALTH CARE FOR THE POOR: COUNTERPOINTS ON PRESERVING MEDICARE

The House Republican Conference vs. Richard A. Gephardt

The House Republican Conference explains and supports legislative initiatives by the Republican Party in the House of Representatives. Richard A. Gephardt is a Democratic congressman from Missouri's Third Congressional District. He is the Democratic Leader in the House of Representatives. The following debate concerns a Republican plan in September of 1995. According to the Associated Press, "The Senate Finance Commit-tee approved a Republican blue-print for massive changes in the government's health programs for America's elderly, poor and disabled. The committee voted the over-haul of Medicare and Medicaid to save $450 billion over the next seven years as part of the GOP's program for balancing the budget by 2002.

■ **POINTS TO CONSIDER**

1. According to Republicans, why is Medicare going broke?

2. How will the "Medicare Preservation Act" protect Medicare?

3. Why is Richard Gephardt opposed to the Republican plan?

4. How do Democrats say a tax cut for the rich is related to Republican attempts to cut Medicare benefits?

Excerpted from "A Summary of the Medicare Preservation Act," House Republican Conference, September 1995, and from a public statement by Richard A. Gephardt with information from the Democratic Senatorial Campaign Committee, September 1995.

STATEMENT BY THE HOUSE REPUBLICAN CONFERENCE

This document details the Medicare Preservation Act (MPA), a comprehensive plan to preserve, protect, and strengthen Medicare, while empowering seniors to choose the health care plan that best suits their needs. The MPA reflects 26 public hearings of the Ways and Means and Commerce Committees, testimony from scores of witnesses, countless meetings with seniors, providers, actuaries, health plan professionals, and town hall meetings across the country.

Medicare is going broke. According to the 1995 report of the Board of Trustees, the outlays of the Hospital Insurance (HI) trust fund will exceed income beginning in 1996, and the trust fund is projected to run out of reserves in 2002.

Not only is the trust fund going broke, but spending growth by the Supplementary Medical Insurance (SMI) trust fund (Part B) is also unsustainable. In 1995, premiums paid by enrollees will finance only about 31.5% of annual costs, according to the 1995 trustees' report. Over the next decade, deficit spending to cover the SMI trust fund will increase from $46 billion in 1995 to $151 billion in 2004, for an average annual growth rate of over 14%.

Mission Statement

The MPA will:

- preserve Medicare to make the program solvent and keep it affordable for current and future generations, while increasing per beneficiary spending from $4,800 in 1995 to $6,700 in 2002.

- protect Medicare to assure beneficiaries that the program as they know it will continue to be available, and

- strengthen Medicare to provide beneficiaries with private coverage options that empower them to choose the health plan that best fits their needs.

Baby Boomer Commission

A Commission on the Effect of the Baby Boom Generation on the Medicare Program will be established to make recommendations to the Congress on the reforms necessary to ensure the preservation of the program, especially in light of anticipated demographic pressures on the program's financing.

Simple Options for Seniors

1. Fee-for-Service Medicare

Beneficiaries will continue to have the right to remain in or return to the public fee-for-service system.

2. MedicarePlus

Under the MedicarePlus reform proposal, the law would be changed to permit a broader array of privately offered plans to be made available to beneficiaries, with the government making premium-type payments to plans on beneficiaries' behalf. These plans could include private traditional insurance, coordinated care, provider-sponsored networks, Medisave plans, and limited enrollment plans sponsored by unions or associations.

a. MedicarePlus Standard Benefits

The Medicare standard benefit package is well-established and the insurance industry is experienced in using it as a reference plan for structuring supplemental benefits and other benefits that HMO plans currently offer to beneficiaries. Under MedicarePlus, we will retain the standard Medicare benefits, so that future beneficiaries will be assured that their benefits will not be reduced if they move to a MedicarePlus plan. If a health plan can provide the Medicare benefits at less than the government contribution, the plan can either provide additional benefits or provide a rebate to beneficiaries up to the amount of the monthly Part B premium. In addition, standardization greatly facilitates competition during open enrollment because it allows beneficiaries to make easy comparisons of plans based on premiums and additional benefits.

The Secretary of Health and Human Services (HHS) will be required to publish annually an information booklet that specifies the available MedicarePlus products and distribute the booklet to all Medicare-eligible individuals. In late 1996, the Department will undertake a major outreach effort to educate beneficiaries on the MedicarePlus options, similar to the annual open season through which government employees choose their health plans.

b. Recognizing Seniors' Differing Health Needs through Government Payments to MedicarePlus Plans

148

Government payments to MedicarePlus health plans will continue to be based on the current practices Medicare uses to pay risk contractors. However, payments will be adjusted to narrow current variations in payment levels across urban and rural markets. The payments will continue to be adjusted to reflect a beneficiary's age and health status as well as local health costs.

c. Protecting Seniors through Tough Standards for MedicarePlus Plans

Any health plan offered to Medicare beneficiaries will have to meet a range of standards, including: market conduct, mode and content of advertising, sales techniques, and related matters; premium and rating rules; consumer protections; reporting and disclosure; enrollment and disenrollment rules; processes for grievances and appeals; requirements for covering emergency and out-of-plan services; service area standards; quality assurance; and financial solvency.

Combating Fraud and Abuse

A top priority of the MPA is to combat Medicare fraud and abuse by rewarding seniors who discover and report fraud and abuse, and by increasing the punishments for those who engage in fraud. We will do this by giving the Secretary of HHS authority to reward seniors who provide information on fraudulent or abusive practices or providers, creating stiff penalties against any MedicarePlus plan that engages in fraud, and increasing civil penalties.

Relief from Excessive Regulation

Current excessive regulations represent a barrier to the efficient delivery of necessary health care services, especially in the managed care area. Providing regulatory relief will improve efficiency and help stem the growth in health care costs. In addition, the MPA provides anti-trust relief and clarifies current safe harbor rules for certain business arrangements.

Medical Malpractice Reform

The threat of abusive malpractice suits drives up health care costs for doctors and patients. The average physician has a 40% chance of being sued at some time in his or her career. Medical malpractice premiums alone now total $10 billion annually. The costs of "defensive medicine" run another $20 to $25 billion a year.

The MPA will cap non-economic damage awards in malpractice cases at $250,000; limit a defendant's liability for non-economic damages to his or her proportionate share of the fault; and limit punitive damages to no more than three times the amount of damages to a claimant for economic loss, or $250,000, whichever is greater.

Guaranteeing Medicare's Continued Solvency

The MPA creates a failsafe mechanism, under which the Secretary of Health and Human Services would annually project Medicare fee-for-service expenditures for the following year, for eight service categories. If projected increases in spending are in excess of targeted growth rates, the Secretary will reduce provider payment updates to ensure that spending growth meets those targets. This mechanism will guarantee continuation of services to beneficiaries and will help protect them from future increases in cost-sharing attributable to excessive spending increases.

STATEMENT BY RICHARD A. GEPHARDT

I want to thank each and every one of you for joining us today — for taking part in this special hearing, on the Republicans' plan to cut Medicare to pay for tax breaks for the wealthy. I have to admit that I had hoped today's hearing would not be necessary. I had hoped that by this day — just weeks before Congress votes on Medicare cuts that will literally shape the future of American health care — the Republican leadership would have scheduled full and substantive hearings on their unprecedented cuts — Or at least shared the details of their Medicare cuts with the American people.

The fact is, even rank-and-file Republican members of Congress have to learn about this secret plan by reading the newspaper. One House Republican said this week that his own staff was — and I quote — "hungering for the details." But Speaker Gingrich and Bob Dole have decided that when it comes to the future of Medicare — when it comes to the seniors who depend on it, the hospitals that survive because of it, the families that would be bankrupted without it — The details should be hidden; the debate should be smothered; and democracy should be denied. After all, you can't protest something you don't even know about. No wonder people are so cynical about this Republican Congress.

Speaker Gingrich held a big news conference — supposedly to share some details of his so-called "plan." But all we got were more patchwork promises, more hemming and hawing, and enough holes to make a swiss cheese. That's why we can't even talk about the details of the Gingrich cuts. I'm not sure they even exist. But there are some things we do know about the Gingrich cuts, and that's what we are going to talk about today — with senior citizens, with the families that may soon have to support them, with doctors and hospital officials — with the flesh-and-blood human beings who will feel the real pain of this health care upheaval.

The Cost

We know that 270 billion dollars is way beyond any estimate of what's needed to make Medicare fully solvent — a fact that some Medicare trustees have taken great pains to express. We know that there is no way to make cuts of that magnitude without hurting real people — by jacking up premiums — by forcing seniors to give up the doctors they've known for decades — by crowding out the kinds of quality care and cutting-edge medical research that save lives.

We know that no matter how you slice it, no matter how you spread these cuts, each and every senior on Medicare will pay — we estimate an average of about 6,700 dollars per person over seven years. If they don't pay through higher costs, they'll pay through worse care, or more sickness and disease. We know that not one red cent of the Republican premium increases on seniors will go back into the Medicare trust fund — even though that's supposed to be the reason for these cuts in the first place.

We know that many hospitals will have to close their doors — some experts estimate as many as 25 percent of all American hospitals — and that will clearly mean the difference between life and death in some communities. We know that the Republicans are using every punishment and inducement they can find to herd seniors into managed care, whether they want it or not — forcing them to give up their own longtime family doctors. We know that you can't ram cuts this deep and dangerous through Congress

151

without a profoundly negative impact on our entire economy — including higher health care costs for businesses, and lower wages for workers. And most importantly of all, we know that if the Republicans would only drop their trickle-down tax breaks, they simply wouldn't need to ravage Medicare.

The Stakes

These are the stakes in this debate. These are the changes the Republicans want to pass by rubber stamp, in about a day — less time than we'd spend on the most routine, nickel-and-dime legislation. The Republicans have closed the door on the kind of full, bipartisan hearings we really need on this issue. They have shut us out of the wood-paneled committee rooms. But they can't stop us from joining the debate. We're going to educate the American people about these cuts — even if we have to do it right here, on the lawn of the Capitol. And then maybe the Republican leadership will understand that if their plan can't survive the bright light of scrutiny, it's time to start treating Medicare less like a tax-cutting candy jar, and more like the sacred commitment it has always been.

Destroy Health Care for Seniors to Pay Off a Tax Cut for the Rich

• The Republican Plan: Cut Medicare for Seniors to Pay Off a Tax Cut for the Rich

Republicans are proposing by far the largest Medicare cut in history to pay off a tax cut for the rich: $270 billion in Medicare cuts to pay for $245 billion in tax cuts for the rich. The Republican argument that their cuts are needed to strengthen Medicare doesn't add up. The bottom line is they're cutting Medicare to pay off the massive tax cuts.

• Who Pays for the Republican Plan? Our Parents and Grandparents

Republicans are cutting Medicare benefits. Under the Republican plan, our parents and grandparents, 37 million people who depend on Medicare, pay more in higher premiums not to make Medicare any stronger but to pay for that tax cut for the rich.

152

- **Senior Citizens Will Pay Much More**

Out of pocket costs could increase thousands of dollars per couple at the end of the Republican's seven year plan to bash Medicare. Medicare premiums will increase $30 a month from $60 to $90 — that means seniors will pay $360 more a year!

- **Senior Citizens Will Get Much Less**

Millions of senior citizens will be forced to give up their doctor. Republican Medicare-bashing will push 500,000 elderly Americans into poverty. Republican plans to transform Medicaid into a block grant will mean that the neediest senior citizens may not be able to get health care coverage because the states where they live won't be able to afford it — unless they raise taxes or cut education spending.

- **Republicans Have Opposed Medicare Since Its Creation. Now They're Going to Save It?**

Thirty years ago, then-Congressman Bob Dole and the majority of Congressional Republicans opposed the creation of Medicare. Ever since, they have regularly tried to cut it. Now they want to destroy it.

- **Democrats Say Strengthen Medicare, Don't Destroy It**

Democrats believe there are improvements that can be made in Medicare to make the system more sound — crack down on waste, fraud and abuse in the system or establish an independent commission to decide how best to improve the program. We want to strengthen Medicare but we're not going to hurt beneficiaries to do it.

153

BIBLIOGRAPHY

Magazine References on the Right:

Bandow, Doug. "Real Term Limits: Now More Than Ever." **Policy Analysis.** 28 Mar.1995.

Carey, Merrick. "Finally, A Two-Sided Environmental Debate." **Human Events.** 17 Feb. 1995: 17.

Cook, Ronald J. "The Religious Schools Controversy." **America.** 18 Feb. 1995: 17-19.

Ferrara, Peter J. and John C. Goodman. "How to Free Elderly from Medicare Shackles." **Human Events.** 12 May 1995: 15.

Henderson, Rick. "Slash and Burn?" **Reason.** May 1995: 45-47.

Higgs, Robert. "How FDR Made the Depression Worse." **The Free Market.** Feb. 1995: 1.

Kincaid, Cliff. "National Public Radio's Pacifica Connection." **Human Events.** 17 Mar. 1995: 4-5.

Olasky, Marvin. "Dismantle the Poverty Punopticon: Pro-Life, Anti-Welfare." **Wall Street Journal.** 22 Mar. 1995: A18.

Robinson, Robert G. "Deficit Delusions." **Reason.** Jan. 1995: 48.

Magazine References on the Left:

Barsamian, David. "Right-Wing Take-Over of Public Broadcasting." **Z Magazine.** Apr. 1995: 6-9.

Chomsky, Noam. "Rollback II: Civilization Marches On." **Z Magazine**. Feb. 1995: 20.

Dowie, Mark. "Greens Outgunned." **Earth Island Journal**. Spring 1995: 26.

Drinan, Robert F. "Affirmative Reactions." **America**. 1 Apr. 1995: 4.

Morrison, Roy. "Contract with Communities." **Toward Freedom**. Apr./May 1995: 11.

"On Contracts and Congress." **Friends Committee on National Legislation, Washington Newsletter**. Feb. 1995.

Rifkin, Jeremy. "Work: A Blueprint for Social Harmony in a World Without Jobs." **Utne Reader**. May/June 1995: 53.

Schor, Juliet B. "The Price We Pay for Abundance." **Business Ethics**. Jan./Feb. 1992: 24.

Swomley, John M. "Profaning This Holy Practice." **Christian Social Action**. Feb. 1995: 25.

Wallis, Jim. "What to Do About the Poor." **Sojourners**. Mar./Apr. 1995: 10.

Woodson, Robert L. "Dismantle the Poverty Panopticon: Anti-Poverty, Pro-Community." **Wall Street Journal**. 22 Mar. 1995: A18.

General Book References

Altemeyer, Bob. **Enemies of Freedom: Understanding Right-Wing Authoritarianism**. Jossey-Bass, 1988.

Anderson, Terry and Donald Leal. **Free Market Environmentalism**. Boulder: West View Press, 1991.

Asimakopulos, A. **Keynes's General Theory and Accumulation**. Cambridge: Cambridge University Press, 1991.

Barash, David P. **The L Word: An Unapologetic, Thoroughly Biased, Long-Overdue Explication and Celebration of Liberalism**. New York: W. Morrow, 1992.

Barnett, Richard J. and John Cavanaugh. **Global Dreams: Imperial Corporations and the New World Order**. New York: Simon & Schuster, 1994.

Belz, Herman. **Equality Transformed: A Quarter Century of Affirmative Action**. London: Transaction Publishers/Social Philosophy and Policy Center, 1991.

Bennet, James T. and Thomas DiLorenzo. **Unhealthy Charities**. New York: Basic Books, 1994.

Blaug, Mark. **John Maynard Keynes: Life, Ideas, Legacy**. New York: St. Martin's Press, 1990.

Bovard, James. **Lost Rights: The Destruction of American Liberty**. New York: St. Martin's Press, 1994.

Chatterjee, Pratap. **The Earth Brokers: Power, Politics and World Development**. New York: Routledge, 1994.

Cornuelle, Richard. **Reclaiming the American Dream: The Role of Private Individuals and Voluntary Association**. New York: Random House, 1965.

Criminal Justice: The Legal System vs. Individual Responsibility. ed. Robert James Bidinotto. Irvington-on-Hudson, New York: Foundation for Economic Education, 1994.

Current Issues in the Economics of Welfare. ed. Nicholas Barr and David Whynes. New York: St. Martin's Press, 1993.

Dasgupta, Partha. **The Control of Resources**. Cambridge: Harvard University Press, 1982.

Devigne, Robert. **Recasting Conservatism: Oakeshott, Strauss, and the Response to Postmodernism**. New Haven: Yale University Press, 1994.

Easterbrook, Gregg. **A Moment on the Earth: The Coming Age of Environmental Optimism**. New York: Viking, 1995.

The Family in Search of a Future: Alternate Models for Moderns. ed. Herbert A. Otto. Appleton-Century-Crofts, 1970.

Garretsen, Harry. **Keynes, Coordination, and Beyond: The Development of Macroeconomic and Nometary Theory Since 1945.** Brookfield, VT: Elgar, 1992.

Gordon, Linda. **Pitied But Not Entitled: Single Mothers and the History of Welfare**. Free Press, 1994.

Gray, John. **Beyond the New Right: Markets, Government and the Common Environment**. New York: Routledge, 1993.

Habermas, Jurgen. **The New Conservatism: Cultural Criticism and the Historians' Debate**. Cambridge: Massachusetts Institute of Technology Press, 1989.

Harbour, William R. **The Foundations of Conservative Thought: An Anglo-American Tradition in Perspective**. South Bend, IN: University of Notre Dame Press, 1982.

Hertzke, Allen D. **Echoes of Discontent: Jesse Jackson, Pat Robertson, and the Resurgence of Populism**. Washington, DC: CQ Press, 1993.

Honderich, Ted. **Conservatism**. Boulder: Westview Press, 1991.

Kates, Don B. **The Second Amendment, Second to None: An Analysis of the Legal Theory and Historical Origins of the Second Amendment**. Second Amendment Foundation, 1982.

Kaufman, Peter Iver. **Redeeming Politics**. Princeton: Princeton University Press, 1990.

Lee, Dwight R. and Richard B. McKenzie. **Failure and Progress: The Bright Side of the Dismal Science**. Washington, DC: Cato Institute, 1993.

Market Liberalism: A Paradigm for the Twenty-First Century. eds. Edward H. Crane and David Boaz. Washington, DC: Cato Institute, 1993.

Olasky, Marvin. **The Tragedy of American Compassion**. Washington, DC: Regnery Publishing, Inc., 1992.

Pettit, Philip. **Judging Justice: An Introduction to Contemporary Political Philosophy**. Boston: Routledge and Kegan Paul, 1980.

Ray, Dixy Lee with Lou Guzzo. **Environmental Overkill**. Washington, DC: Regnery Gateway, 1993.

Regulation: Economic Theory and History. ed. Jack High. Ann Arbor, Michigan: University of Michigan Press, 1991.

Sen, Amartya Kumar. **Inequality Reexamined**. Cambridge: Harvard University Press, 1992.

Sklar, Holly. **Chaos or Community: Seeking Solutions, Not Scapegoats to Bad Economics**. Boston: South End Press, 1995.

Sowell, Thomas. **The Economics of Politics and Race**. New York: Quill, 1983.

Walsh, David. **After Ideology: Recovering the Spiritual Foundations of Freedom**. San Francisco: Harper, 1990.

Ward, Benjamin. **The Ideal Worlds of Economics: Liberal, Radical, and Conservative Economic World Views**. Basic Books, 1979.

INDEX